what do we know and what should we do about...?

housing

Rowland Atkinson
and Keith Jacobs

Los Angeles | London | New Delhi
Singapore | Washington DC | Melbourne

Los Angeles | London | New Delhi
Singapore | Washington DC | Melbourne

SAGE Publications Ltd
1 Oliver's Yard
55 City Road
London EC1Y 1SP

SAGE Publications Inc.
2455 Teller Road
Thousand Oaks, California 91320

SAGE Publications India Pvt Ltd
B 1/I 1 Mohan Cooperative Industrial Area
Mathura Road
New Delhi 110 044

SAGE Publications Asia-Pacific Pte Ltd
3 Church Street
#10-04 Samsung Hub
Singapore 049483

© Rowland Atkinson and Keith Jacobs 2020

First published 2020

Editor: Matthew Waters
Editorial assistant: Jasleen Kaur
Production editor: Katherine Haw
Copyeditor: Neville Hankins
Proofreader: Clare Weaver
Indexer: Charmian Parkin
Marketing manager: George Kimble
Cover design: Lisa Harper-Wells
Typeset by: C&M Digitals (P) Ltd, Chennai, India
Printed in the UK

Library of Congress Control Number: 2019956624

British Library Cataloguing in Publication data

A catalogue record for this book is available from the British Library

ISBN 978-1-5264-6656-3
ISBN 978-1-5264-6655-6 (pbk)

At SAGE we take sustainability seriously. Most of our products are printed in the UK using responsibly sourced papers and boards. When we print overseas we ensure sustainable papers are used as measured by the PREPS grading system. We undertake an annual audit to monitor our sustainability.

contents

titles in the series

about the series

Every news bulletin carries stories which relate in some way to the social sciences – most obviously politics, economics and sociology but also, often, anthropology, business studies, security studies, criminology, geography and many others.

Yet despite the existence of large numbers of academics who research these subjects, relatively little of their work is known to the general public. There are many reasons for that but one, arguably, is that the kinds of formats that social scientists publish in, and the way in which they write, are simply not accessible to the general public.

The guiding theme of this series is to provide a format and a way of writing which addresses this problem. Each book in the series is concerned with a topic of widespread public interest, and each is written in a way which is readily understandable to the general reader with no particular background knowledge.

The authors are academics with an established reputation and a track record of research in the relevant subject. They provide an overview of the research knowledge about the subject, whether this be long-established or reporting the most recent findings; widely accepted or still controversial. Often in public debate there is a demand for greater clarity about the facts, and that is one of the things the books in this series provide.

However, in social sciences, facts are often disputed and subject to different interpretations. They do not always, or even often, 'speak for themselves'. The authors therefore strive to show the different interpretations or the key controversies about their topics, but without getting bogged down in arcane academic arguments.

Not only can there be disputes about facts but also there are almost invariably different views on what should follow from these facts. And, in any case, public debate requires more of academics than just to report facts; it is also necessary to make suggestions and recommendations about the implications of these facts.

Thus each volume also contains ideas about 'what we should do' within each topic area. These are based upon the authors' knowledge of the field but also, inevitably, upon their own views, values and preferences. Readers may not agree with them, but the intention is to provoke thought and well-informed debate.

Chris Grey, Series Editor

Professor of Organization Studies

Royal Holloway, University of London

about the authors

Rowland Atkinson is Research Chair in Inclusive Societies at the University of Sheffield. His work focuses on housing and city life, with a particular emphasis on inequalities and social divisions. His most recent publications include: *Alpha City* (Verso 2020), *Urban Criminology* (with Gareth Millington, Routledge 2018), *Domestic Fortress* (with Sarah Blandy, Manchester University Press 2016) and *House, Home and Society* (with Keith Jacobs, Palgrave 2016).

Keith Jacobs is Professor of Sociology at the University of Tasmania. His most recent publications include: an edited collection with Jeff Malpas, *Philosophy and the City: Interdisciplinary and Transcultural Perspectives* (Rowman and Littlefield 2019), *Neoliberal Housing Policy: An International Perspective* (Routledge 2019) and *House, Home and Society* (co-authored with Rowland Atkinson, Palgrave 2016).

acknowledgements

For their enormous help in critiquing and honing the arguments presented here we want to thank our editor, Chris Grey; and colleagues, Tony Manzi, Ryan Powell and Paul Watt.

We have always been aware that academic scholarship is a collective endeavour and that ideas are derived from different sources, but we wish to highlight the influence on us of a book published some 44 years ago by Peter Ambrose and Bob Colenutt, namely the really excellent, *The Property Machine.*

We have also drawn inspiration from the more recent and insightful contributions on the housing crisis by Duncan Bowie, Danny Dorling, Nick Gallent, David Madden, Peter Marcuse and Anna Minton.

Dedicated to the provision of homes for all, not houses for profit.

introduction

One thing that we seem to know very clearly about housing is that something is very badly wrong with it. Whether it be its cost, its availability, its production or its suitability, housing is in a state of continuing crisis on so many different levels. The form of this crisis can be seen in the UK – in rising homelessness, overcrowding, squalor in the private rented sector, rising mortgage debts, beds in sheds, and inadequate rate of constructing new housing for those desperately in need of it. This much is clear, and most people, regardless of their personal politics, are able to see that a massive social need for stable, appropriate and affordable homes is not being met. Yet this crisis has been with us in some form or another for well over a century. Our task in this book is to highlight the enduring nature of this crisis and to throw light on why resolving it remains unlikely given the powerful interests involved.

The government's recent White Paper *Fixing our Broken Housing Market* (Department of Communities and Local Government, 2017) conveys the impression that it is serious about taking action and that nothing short of radical reform is required. However, there is no acknowledgement of how the housing system establishes and reinforces wealth inequality. Instead, the paper suggests that the UK's housing problem can be identified in a lack of sufficient housing. We are told that 'the problem is threefold: not enough local authority planning for the homes they need; house building that is simply too slow; and a construction industry that is too reliant on a small number of big players'. Further on it is stated with confidence that 'the cause of our housing shortage is simple enough – not enough homes are being built. Fixing it is more complex. This is a problem that has built up over many years, and solving it requires a radical re-think of our whole approach to home building'. So, the fix is in fact not radical but little more than a set of policy interventions that 'comes down to planning for building homes in the right places, faster and diversifying the market to open up opportunities for small builders'.

The 2017 White Paper received qualified praise from some quarters. For example, the housing pressure group Shelter acknowledged that the publication is 'an important step and it is encouraging to see a change from demand side to supply side interventions with the intention of getting more homes and more affordable homes built' (Shelter, 2017: 3). However, Shelter went on to note that a new system is required, 'one that is focused on delivering community benefit ahead of profit' (p. 4). As we argue in this book, we also see the urgency of a restructured housing system but, unlike the government, we want to encourage readers to look at the 'broken housing market' in a different way. In particular, we suggest that another way of considering these enormous problems would be to see them, not as a consequence of mismanagement or a policy shortfall (though they are partly that), but instead as evidence of the healthy operation of a system delivering good returns to already wealthy and powerful individuals and institutions.

The housing system's primary beneficiaries are not ordinary citizens but rather banks and developers, landlords, speculative investors, the majority of homeowners and real estate agencies. This constellation of interests, referred to here as the property machine, has persistently left human need unaddressed through its pursuit of profit and electoral advantage. What we highlight in this book is that these key actors and institutions benefit enormously from a housing system that is carefully managed politically in order that the interests of the property sector are met. Why should these needs be met above all others? Put bluntly this is because the pursuit of profit by this sector has long been central to the idea (not the reality) that a well-functioning economy is one based on investment in and the circulation of property. Such circulation generates significant gains for the wealthy and powerful whose interests are entwined with significant parts of the political system. The property sector is narrowly construed as comprising builders and developers (and perhaps social and public housing providers). The idea of a property machine helps us to see that a much broader system of interests and alliances encompasses governments, banks and other financial institutions alongside builders, landlords and developers. If we extend our analytical frame in this way we begin to understand how this machine will operate in ways that seek out an orderly approach that maintains good returns to its powerful components.

Many people who feel that they know something about today's housing problems often argue, wrongly, that the fundamentals of supply need to be recognised first. From such a position, it is often argued, we can then begin to look after those whom the market fails in terms of a basic lack of housing or its high cost due to its relative scarcity. Yet what we have seen historically, particularly over the past 40 years, is that whether the economy is faring well or poorly, there has been a systematic assault on the position of and provision for poorer households. One of the most pernicious aspects of such a system is that the majority of households own or are buying their home. Ownership is not bad in its own right but what it does do is to create a set of sectional interests and incentives – to see house prices rise (even if owners do not always benefit from this, as we argue later), to maintain house building at levels that enable rises in the value of these assets and to maintain a macroeconomic setting that helps with house price rises (low interest rates and incentives to prospective buyers alongside weak attempts at addressing intergenerational housing wealth inheritance).

Placating homeowners and, increasingly, owners who have become landlords has long been important to strategies to achieve electoral success and to substitute the role of the state (in terms of welfare and pensions) for the promise of wealth that can be used to fund retirement and good lifestyles. Sales of public housing (the Right to Buy) have also been important to this story of a thinning of the state's response and governments on both right and left have done little to challenge the apparent needs of owners, the demands of the property sector and the need for secure social housing that can be accessed affordably.

It is possible to think that governments are concerned about homelessness, ill-health from poor conditions, hard-pressed tenants paying exorbitant rents and the many who struggle to pay for their homes. This is a naive, if understandable, view. Such a view comes from a willingness to accept that occasional crumbs of comfort will fall to those who are desperately in need but that deeper reform is either impossible or undesirable. It is, for example, possible to find numerous examples of homeowner programmes, discounts and subsidies for new buyers, for rough sleeper initiatives and for pronouncements by government officials that something must be done about slow planning systems and for increased supply. Yet such responses are weak, often fleeting and, worst of all, do nothing to address the structural flaws of a system designed to advantage the already wealthy.

If we really want to understand housing as a human right and to ensure that the utter despair and terrible stress of being housed in poor conditions, living long distances from work and schooling opportunities or at intense cost are addressed, then we need a more incisive and deeper approach that rejects the superficial responses that many continue to offer. Such an approach does not require revolutionary socialism (though some will of course argue this way forward), but it *will* require those with plenty to have less, for prospective inheritors to see less generous windfalls, for prospective owners that they will have to save rather than being gifted subsidies, for public housing to be built rather than supporting profit-motivated private landlordism and for the very profitable property sector to act more clearly in line with the needs of the many. If this initial sketch appears to be a radical programme of sorts then we are happy for it to be described as such.

Our purpose in this book is to cut through the noise of a lot of the debate and false leads in how we assess the problem of housing people securely, affordably and comfortably. Later on, we will try to outline some reform proposals but suggest from the outset that many readers, policymakers and politicians will cast these as not only unworkable but also extreme. We take aim, not at some abstract notion of capitalism, but rather at the way that the architecture of politics, economy and society creates a distinctive set of imperatives and incentives that privilege capitalist actors and institutions. Our challenge to the reader is this: are you ready to accept that you, your political system and a set of vested interests (of capital and those co-opted to be the cogs of such a system) may be working against the resolution of the housing crisis? Would you be prepared to sacrifice some of your privilege and wealth so that all can enjoy a better home?

Our arguments stand on the shoulders of work done by many of our colleagues and the clear evidence base they have produced over time. This work helps us to disentangle the roots of the housing problem and ways forward to address it. *To place our argument up front – we suggest that the way that housing is provided, bought, sold and created operates within a system that by design and by political management delivers dividends to the wealthiest and most powerful in society.* Yet much of what is written about housing often suggests the need for some particular fix – such as through more philanthropy, better services for homeless people, less gentrification, more joined-up responses between agencies, more diversity and, of course, more housing in general. None of these answers are wrong, but they mistake symptoms and outcomes in terms of the way that housing is produced and resourced in our society, instead of thinking about the concerted responses that would be required to make more reasonable housing outcomes a reality. In this sense increasingly frank debates are needed that prevent dissembling, obfuscating evidence and arguments for housing that are frequently a cover for business as usual – business that sees those with most gaining still further.

Where we depart from some of the more recent contributions to the housing debate is that we see little or no benefit in trying to reach a consensus with, or accommodation of, the powerful interests that have carefully sought to position themselves on the side of low-income households and the dispossessed through marketing campaigns or through cautious arguments. We would suggest that banks, developers, real estate agencies have a stake in maintaining the conditions for housing scarcity and for inflating the value of these assets while being careful to appear to the wider public as being sympathetic to progressive reform. Many of these marketing efforts have worked well. Over the last 30 years or so, many housing campaigners have thought it necessary to work alongside powerful industry agencies and that some progress can be achieved through this co-operation. Yet it is increasingly clear that very little has been achieved.

The prospects of many low-income households have deteriorated considerably while the opportunities for profiteering through speculative forms of housing investment have accelerated dramatically. This can be witnessed in the ways in which the property sector has increasingly deregulated and 'financialised'[1] by allowing greater amounts to be borrowed by buyers (which has helped prices to rise), through the use of mortgages as the basis of new financial products, by arguing for the cutting of planning 'red tape' while holding construction at slow rates and by increasing work with weak local governments to promote plans for gentrification and the destruction of public housing. Homelessness is now more evident in many UK cities and conditions in the private rental market are for many of very high cost, of poor quality and insecure.

What we call the housing system is composed of competing interests which jostle to make as much money as possible, with the state broadly helping in this process since it understands that these interests are part of its core constituency of supporters and that their actions help to build a thriving economy. The housing system is embedded in the financial systems that operate in the UK but also in the ways that government welfare services are delivered. As we argue, the homeless and many low-income tenants living in private rental and public housing stock have been subjected to a set of punitive welfare policies that have been purposefully designed to blame individuals for their problems and public housing as a failed tenure. Alongside these cuts the assistance of landlords and owners has been significant even while many now strongly critique the idea that property wealth, its circulation and rising price are signs of a healthy economy, not least because it is prone to periods of crisis alongside inadequately providing for those in need.

As we get further into this, we will see how these understandings fall short of understanding the more complex impact, or curse, of finance facilitated in large part by the market in houses. Most housing in the UK is allocated through market mechanisms – if you have the money you can buy a house and often will make money once it is sold (often because successive generations entering the system borrow increasing amounts of money to get onto the so-called housing ladder). What all of this means in practice is a system in which many jostle to achieve the economic rewards that appear to flow from ownership, understanding that to rent is to be locked out of these potential windfalls. In other countries with more stabilising housing policies and more secure rental systems, homeownership can look much less attractive to the extent that the idea of investing to make money, rather than to use and live in that housing, makes little or no sense. Facing down the widely held idea that ownership offers a vehicle to personal wealth while those outside the sector suffer is something that requires urgent attention.

Our hope is that a more open and accurate understanding of the housing system can be generated, based on the primary principle of seeking fair and good outcomes for all. The goal here is to help generate widely shared understandings of how particular narratives or stories about the root of housing problems have become engrained in social and political conversations while others are denigrated or shot down. As we discuss in subsequent chapters, successive governments have been active agents in sustaining a narrative of the housing system that has had the effect of actively accentuating wealth inequalities in the UK through its support for commodified forms of housing (through the planning system and tax subsidies to landlords and homeowners) while demonising and indeed destroying the role of public housing. Many governments have continued to forecast that the housing problems of the contemporary UK are a temporary aberration that are amenable to managerial tinkering rather than more fundamental and incisive structural reform.

If we take a historical view, we can see that the housing crisis is a recurring and persistent phenomenon. Taking such a view enables us to understand how very similar interests and mechanisms have allowed the wealthy and property intermediaries to secure continued profits while leaving root conditions unchanged. One of the core assumptions that underpins this book is that history offers a strong guide to making sense of the housing system of today and the problematic legacies that endure. It is through historical reflection that we are able to establish the connections that sustain contemporary housing inequalities focused around the axes of generations, tenure and wealth. A reflection on the past also provides us with evidence of policy reforms that have been successful. As we explain, many of the necessary steps that would be needed to ameliorate the contemporary UK housing crisis have as their antecedent the interventions achieved particularly in the two decades following the Second World War with the rapid rise of public housing.

Something is very wrong in the housing system, depending on whose voice one represents. Yet everyone appears to know the answer. The builders know it is the planning system that holds up construction. The planners know that the builders would never dream of price-deflating building rates because it would dent their profits. Progressive analysts know that the system is built to ensure profits for landlords, banks and builders and that consumers will never win or indeed be satisfied. But the general situation is made worse in a context in which the property sector has helped to financialise the home – building and investing on behalf of the affluent, pension funds and investors rather than seeing their role as ensuring a well-housed, cohesive community. And why should they? They are profit-making entities in a competitive market. Yet in reality this market is steered and managed by macroeconomic policies that generate windfalls to the wealthiest, co-ordinated by a political system that works in concert with the majority of the population who control capital, own property or seek to join these groups.

The deeper point is perhaps increasingly obvious: that only state co-ordination, accountable decision-making and public housing can complement the role of homeownership as the means by which housing problems are resolved and an escape from over-priced private landlord-ism can be achieved. In open competitions for core housing resources those with the greatest wealth will win out and it is this class that has been winning for a long time.

Note

1. This is an important term and refers to the rising influence of markets and investment in an ever-increasing range of products, services and elements of everyday life. Housing is a particularly good example of such processes in action as investment funds, banks and other institutions not only borrow, lend and invest but also create additional financial instruments and products on the back of this debt which can also be bought and sold to create new invest-ment opportunities. Also rolled into such ideas is the attempt to make into an asset anything that can be. Here, the use of public housing as a new potential source of profitable investment activity is a notable additional element of such financialisation – homes that could not be bought or sold were made available to tenants under Right to Buy policy and now investment funds are looking to get involved in the running of public housing.

the background

Introduction

As we have explained so far, our core argument is that the housing crisis is a notable outcome of the working of the property machine as it is currently constituted. This is a state of affairs that we must grasp in order to critically consider and use to explain the state of housing today, and the kind of response that might flow from this. But what is particularly important to note is that any political response to the crisis needs to be system-focused rather than piecemeal. In this chapter we trace some of the key social and economic forces and the broad range of policies that have shaped and responded to the UK's housing crisis. We show how the roots of key current problems such as homelessness, the lack of affordable housing and insecurity in the private rental sector can be located in the choices made by successive governments to prioritise the interests of capital above social need.

Capitalism is characterised not simply by a system of private property (though this is key to the claims of the rich and powerful to continued streams of income) but also in a commitment to continuing economic expansion. The benefits of such a system flow unevenly to those who already control capital – money that seeks to increase its 'mass', and resources such as housing or shares, from which resources can flow indefinitely. Ownership of a home to rent, a factory to produce goods or intellectual property (such as a platform like Uber) enable immense flows of money and profit back to those who own these means of production, ownership or utilities. This is a distinctive system and one that generates significant powers and interests at the heart of the political process tied to it. One example of this political connection to the structures of our economy can be seen in the housing system itself since this is an economy understood as something defined by interests and legal titles that establish notions of property but also ideas about legitimate economic activity and profit making from those resources. The state's commitment to underwrite and facilitate these activities is important.

Our analysis highlights the need to understand how it is that housing, property, law, finance and construction form a constellation of interests and powerful actors whose job it is for politics and government to arbitrate across and to support. Planners, to take one example, are also linked to this system since they must seek to support public interests but also enable profit-making capital ventures through the granting of rights to land and for development capitalists to secure profits and incomes from building on it. This tension between public interests and capital is particularly evident in debates about greenfield development and in relation to the provision (or lack of it) of affordable and social housing in new developments.

Historically, housing policymakers in government meanwhile have presided over a system that favours landlords foremost, owner occupiers and a waning interest in non-market housing provided for or at arm's length by the state. Seen in this way, the political system offers some insight into the ranged interests of different sections of capital that have similar but varying interests. There are the real estate capitalists (a group that includes developers, builders, bankers) with an interest in building, selling and renting properties; those capitalists who own land or who are landlords (private landlords, landed aristocrats and new landholders like sovereign wealth funds and investors which may also include pension companies and private investment funds); and industrial capitalists (including companies and manufacturing interests) who would prefer to see affordable homes so that their employees can live cheaply and thus not demand higher wages! These competing interests vary but all input into the political system through their own lobbying activities; the apparent alignment of their interests (many politicians seek to respond to the needs of particular sections of capital, others end up on corporate boards of construction and other companies, act as company advisers and work for banks and accountancy companies); their votes and those of the people and institutions they represent.

Capitalism and the housing crisis

Situating the housing interventions of the state requires us to examine the ideological and political context of their formation. In order to understand housing policy, we need to make sense of the contemporary housing crisis, not as something that has somehow landed or occurred in some unfortunate way, but in a way that is deeply rooted in the distinctive system of interests of which it is ultimately a part. The continued pursuit of profitability (seeking to generate maximum returns on investment) is central to the capitalist system. Residential housing is particularly attractive for investors, because there is a shortage of stock and the fact that everyone needs a home ensures demand is constant. A persistent shortage helps profit rates to be high and thus also attract investors who are more than happy to see high returns, even if this ultimately immiserates entire populations, like those renting privately. Unlike other forms of investment, property speculation in existing homes is relatively straightforward and it requires no productive investment in labour or machinery. Trading in homes requires little more than an investor having access to sufficient capital (which can be borrowed or inherited or created via the pooled resources of investors into property funds) to pay for the cost of a property and make money from both renting the property to a household and selling the property on at a time when the value of the home has increased.

It was Marx's patron and collaborator Friedrich Engels who recognised that, 'as long as the capitalist mode of production continues to exist, it is folly to hope for an isolated solution to the housing question or of any other social question affecting the fate of workers' (Engels, 1872). Engels was adamant that landlords who owned and rented their properties were effectively sourcing their profits from the productive labour of those who paid them rent. In short, landlords' profits were not earned through their own work but simply due to their good fortune in owning property.[1] More recently, scholars like David Harvey (2010) and Thomas Piketty (2014) have extended Engels' analysis by showing how housing not only provides shelter to workers but also operates as an asset to generate wealth among a few who control its ownership and sale, or to those who rent it out. For the speculative investor (and indeed speculative homeowner!), there are potential profits to be made by speculating on the future value of a house and these opportunities have been abetted by governments who have sought to protect profit by maintaining low interest rates or by giving preferential taxation arrangements to landlords or homeowners.[2]

Finance is an embedded element of the provision and consumption of homes, but it is also an increasing problem insofar as it represents a set of interests that disregards human need and works hard to maximise profits. One might say that this would not be a problem were it not for the increasing aggressivity and permitted role of finance capital in the construction or renting of homes, its extended role in buying and managing social housing and its underwriting of inflating house prices through lax lending practices. These developments have been encouraged by successive governments supportive of these trends towards financialisation. This has had the effect of strengthening the power of the financial sector based in London and which many politicians, civil servants and indeed many others have come to view as a critical component of the national economy despite its lack of productivity or social value.

Some commentators who have explored the influence of finance (Shaxson, 2018) now draw attention to what they see as a quite malign influence and its problematic impact on the UK and other national economies. For example, some banking institutions and financiers have successfully used offshore subsidiaries and shadow banking arrangements to avoid paying tax liabilities on housing – using shell companies to anonymously buy billions of pounds' worth of property and to extract the profits from these sales offshore. This speculative form of investment has great appeal to financiers but it has made it much harder for productive industries that employ labour to secure investment funds to grow their business (Piketty, 2014).

The impact of these developments has generated significant and new forms of inequality that revolve particularly around whether individuals draw their income from capital (and the revenues that stem from rents on property or shares in it) or from their own work, as well as whether they own their own (or additional) properties or rent their home. Housing wealth is now an important element of an emerging landscape of social class in the UK that analysts are only beginning to identify. These developments have generated what economists would themselves describe as inefficient and failing markets. This is because, as capital has been allowed to become more involved in the provision of housing, its profit-maximising goals have tended to lead to poor-quality homes, the highest rents that can be demanded, rising house prices, the massing of construction activity in 'hot' markets rather than where or who it is most needed for (notably the south-east) and the general failure to house (affordably or adequately) those on low incomes. It is also increasingly evident that an internationali- sation of finance means that many such institutions now seek to operate schemes through which value and profit are spirited away from those on lower incomes and national economies through clever tax-avoiding and tax-evading schemes, via offshore investment trusts and opaque account- ing practices which flow back to those with capital.

The increasing role of finance and capital in the provision of housing has accentuated its role as an asset class, a thing for investment and trade. Today, the performance of these assets, whether prices are going up or not, has become a significant preoccupation for governments and owners. This has led to governments safeguarding housing's role as an exchange good to enhance investment returns and profits. One key effect of this situation has been the amplification of wealth inequality in the UK and other simi- lar nation states – notably countries like the United States, Spain, Greece, Ireland and even countries like the Netherlands and Germany which had tended to celebrate the role of public housing while using policies that tended to moderate the role of housing as a source of investment gains.

Housing is tied to much larger systems of wealth accumulation that have generated enormous gains to those who own capital in the form of shares, savings and, of course, property. Piketty's (2014) influential analy- sis highlighted that the holders of capital have, in the post-war period, consistently made more from the returns on their capital than those work- ing. Some inkling of this reward system at work can be seen in cities like London where the rapid appreciation of house prices meant that owners and landlords of these properties were 'earning' more from these increases than someone working for a living (Minton, 2017). This property is part of a system that yields enormously uneven rewards and those with little or no housing wealth are locked out of these systems.

Speculative investment in housing has been a development across the global economy, linked to major economic transformations that took place from around the 1980s. These transformations included policy and regulatory measures advanced by nation states that involved the deregu- lation of finance and lending controls so that borrowing increased and relatively small amounts of existing wealth could be used to enlarge prop- erty portfolios and profits. What is important about this financial circuit of purchasing and returns is that it involves no productive form of labour or industry but rather the circulation and expansion of money in search of still greater returns. In many cases this has encouraged investors to move funds from productive capital (in the production of various good and services) to the deployment of such investment in speculation on shares, currencies, futures markets and commodities such as oil and assets like housing. Housing itself has become a major circuit involving purchasing, sale, construction and the building of massive rental portfolios to drive returns to investors.

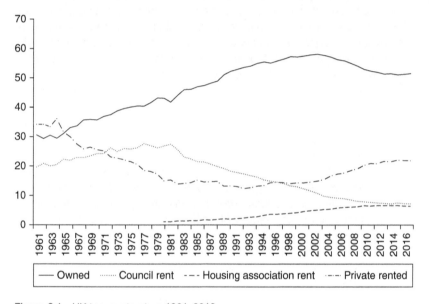

Figure 2.1 UK tenure structure 1961–2016

Source: ONS, Resolution foundation data

The housing crisis is a constitutive feature of capitalist economic cycles of boom and bust which reappear as over-investment in property leads to crashes and as investment motives undermine important social goals. Housing is also implicated in creating forms of class position that appear around particular tenurial and capital/sectional interests – of capital and labour and the stratification that takes form within these groups (Harvey, 2010). Here we can see how inequalities have become increasingly focused around housing as well as enormous wage inequalities that have been accentuated by the actions of successive UK governments to reduce the capacity of trade unions to secure living or fairer wages through collective bargaining. A household's tenurial position (broadly, whether an owner or renter) significantly shapes a wide range of social and economic outcomes and whose relative number has shifted dramatically over time with the dominance of owner occupation falling back alongside a deeper loss of public housing and the rise of private renting in tandem with the incentives to invest in this sector (see Figure 2.1). While curbing wage increases may have put downward pressure on inflation, it has also required workers to become hugely indebted to lending institutions as they sought to secure a home – through longer loan terms and riskier, higher loan to value ratios (also implicated in subsequent rounds of repossession which generated expanded portfolios to many investors who snapped up these assets cheaply).

Today, conditions remain in place both for investors to make significant profits from housing assets and for banks to generate wealth from lending money to households. It should come as no surprise that individual household debt in the UK (both debt in relation to the home and so-called unsecured debt which involves other loans and credit cards) has risen considerably over the last 30 years. In 2019, UK homeowners owed an average of £15,000 in unsecured debt and nearly 1% (0.79%) of owners with mortgages are in arrears (Brignall, 2019). All of this presents systemic risks which fall to governments, rather than banks and other lenders, to resolve where a crisis point is reached. As the financial crisis of 2008 highlighted, government will always tend to identify its role as favouring the needs of the financial system rather than private households (the choice taken was to throw money at shoring up the position of the banks and the gifting of cheap money through quantitative easing while cutting the cost of public services to avoid raising taxes), though of course the systemic shock generated by a deepening financial crisis would indeed have been a potentially terrifying event.

We should not be surprised that businesses, such as real estate agencies, banks, developers and builders, take active steps to protect their profits. For each of these industries, scarcity in the housing market is a very helpful precondition for maintaining and boosting profits. Businesses will always seek to maximise their profit by charging the highest possible price that consumers are willing to pay and will tend to limit supply when necessary to raise profits further. What is also interesting to note is the role of government as a kind of risk carrier when crises occur (bailing out banks) as well as its role in opening new markets and commercial opportunities for capital (such as allowing private investors to purchase social housing).

The UK government, as we have explained, has prioritised the interests of commercial institutions by resisting pressures to reform the tax system or committing sufficient funds available to build new social housing. Instead, the government engages in continually rhetorical forms of policy-making – identifying housing shortages as a problem while then stepping back from committing sufficient resources to address this shortage. UK government housing policy in effect becomes *aspirational* rather than *actual*. The intent is to convey a *sense* of action and purposefulness to assuage sections of the electorate who do not invest in property that their needs are being addressed as possible concerted action is pushed ever further down the line. It is these continued policy decisions which underpin our insistence that it is a categorical error to view the contemporary housing crisis as a temporary aberration or one where, in a short time period, market equilibrium will be restored so that housing becomes affordable.

Trends in housing policy

The 1950s–1970s

Offering a systemic analysis partly rests on identifying long-term trends. We can see through a slightly more historical perspective how, throughout the post-war period, governments have often intervened to promote the commodification of housing by expanding homeownership – making a required social need and good into a tradable asset. Up until the late 1970s private landlordism was generally recognised by all political parties as a problematic tenure that had negative effects for low-income households (see again Figure 2.1). While there were differences regarding the funding of council house building programmes during this period, both Labour and the Conservatives recognised its role in protecting households from the vagaries of the private market and also abetting the labour market by establishing stability.

The late 1940s to the mid-1970s marked a sustained period of council house building to replace inner city privately owned slums. Many of the new council flats were system-built high-density dwellings. While Labour and Conservative policies did differ, there was an understanding that public housing was an effective way to meet 'the traditional aim of a decent home for all families at a price within their means' (Department of the Environment, 1971: 1). Much of the investment in council housing at this time directly benefitted large private sector developers and concerns about falling levels of profitability in the private building industry were an influence on the policies of governments to resource large, system-built council housing estates (Dunleavy, 1981; Wellings, 2006). Another way of thinking about this is to suggest that the state's support for capital was channelled, at least insofar as housing was concerned, through the construction of municipal homes made available to all.

Another compelling explanation for the funding of public housing during this period was that housing tended to be

> provided in capitalist societies in commodified forms...only when adequate provision in commodified form is not possible (even with state support) and when this situation has some broader significance for the dominant social and economic order, that recourse is made to large-scale, partially decommodified, state-subsidized and politically controlled 'mass' social rented housing. (Harloe, 1995: 6)

In this view, the bipartisan support for council housing was both a pragmatic and economic policy used to place downwards pressure on collective wage bargaining by keeping housing costs low, and to ensure labour productivity was not undermined by housing insecurity while also offering good contracts to private developers. It is tempting to think of council housing provision as a genuine response to distress in the private sector. While this is certainly how politicians have often explained their interventions in the housing market, a more plausible explanation is that concerns about the UK's economy and the profitability of the construction industry in particular were primary drivers.

The mid-1970s to mid-1990s

The 1970s was a period of high inflation and falling levels of productivity. Keynesian-inspired economic policymaking which stressed public invest-ment to boost the economy was increasingly seen as generating inflationary pressures. At this time, even a Labour administration (1974–1979) took steps to stem wage rises and cut public expenditure as a way to enhance UK industrial competitiveness. Ideologues within the Conservative opposition also saw an opportunity to align their party with values such as freedom, choice and enterprise. In this respect housing was an important element of this ideological position. Rewarding homeowners was seen as politically expedient and the vehicle to achieve this was newly introduced 'Right to Buy' policies for council tenants and generous tax reliefs for homeowners. It was in the aftermath of the Conservative Party election victory in 1979 that council housing repairs and renewal expenditure were significantly cut and funds were then switched to more demand-side interventions, such as individual assistance to low-income households in the form of housing benefit and discounts for tenants who bought their council home.

The promotion of homeownership that was a feature of Conservative governments would probably not have been so effective had council housing been properly funded. But the idea that there should be government support for a level playing field of choices between tenures was anathema to a party that was committed to a vision of private ownership, a popular set of policies that more or less masked the reality that the deeper interests and beneficiaries were embodied by capital itself. So, a strategy to reduce the appeal of council housing was put in effect. We can find evidence for this from the late 1970s onwards, whereby council housing was effectively recast as a 'residual' tenure – presented as one that was not chosen and also one that should be designated only to those in acute need.

The government passed legislation (the 1980 Housing Act and 1984 Local Government Finance Act) that extended the 'Right to Buy' provisions available to council tenants but also curtailed the capacity of local authorities to build new stock. Expenditure cuts impacted on councils' repair and maintenance budgets; for the government this was a relatively easier option to make savings as the impact of these cuts would only be experienced in later years. The scale of cuts imposed on public housing was disproportionally high compared with other areas of welfare spending. It was estimated that 75% of the total cuts in all government spending in the 1970s were focused on repairs and maintenance budgets set aside for local authorities (Malpass and Murie, 1994: 107).

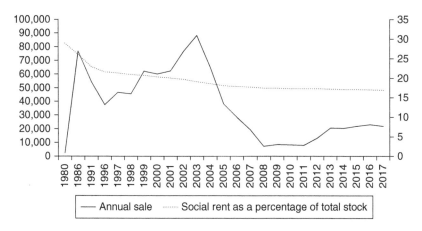

Figure 2.2   Annual sales of English local authority homes 1980–2017

Source: MHCLG/Resolution Foundation

In Figure 2.2, the annual sales of council homes (left Y axis) are juxtaposed with the overall size of the social rented sector (local authority and housing associations) in England (right Y axis). The figure highlights how sales and inadequate investment have left this sector much smaller and less able to meet the accommodation needs of low-income households.

The 1980 Housing Act has an enduring impact for housing policy debates today. The Act forced local authorities to provide large discounts to encourage council tenants to buy their home and for these proceeds to flow to central government in a privatisation that raised more money than North Sea oil in its first 20 years for the state. At the start of this period, there were as many as 6.5 million council properties in the UK with one in three households renting their home from a local authority. As we have noted, council housing was seen as a stable, cheaper and better quality option than the private rental market (Murie, 2018). The Right to Buy featured in the 1979 Conservative Party's general election campaign and undoubtedly helped to secure votes in many Labour strongholds and as many as 1 million properties were sold in the

1980s (Pawson and Mullins, 2010). But the Right to Buy was not the only housing policy during the 1980s that assisted the Conservative Party. There is also evidence that empty council stock was purposefully sold off to gain electoral advantage in local council elections. In the London Borough of Westminster, the Conservative council leader, Dame Shirley Porter, introduced an initiative known as 'Building safer communities'. The governing party hoped the initiative would help protect its slim majority in marginal wards by ensuring that vacated council homes were sold to new owners, rather than re-let to incoming tenants who they thought would probably vote for the Labour Party (Hoskens, 2007).

The Right to Buy certainly benefitted many of the households who bought their home, but as the properties that sold were not replaced by new stock, the total number of council house lettings declined from 221,000 in 2001 to 83,000 in 2013/14 (Murie, 2018). Legislation passed in 1989 (The Local Government and Housing Act) imposed rules that stopped local councils using revenue from non-housing sources to subsidise the rents paid by council tenants. The effect of this policy was to increase the cost of renting to nearer the rents charged by landlords in the private rental sector. In practice, the increase in rents charged by local authorities acted as a further incentive for tenants to buy their home.

The commodification of public housing though initiatives such as the Right to Buy was part of a larger ideological project that conflated forms of free enterprise, property and capital with the interests of those who lacked any real wealth. These were in many ways clever and popular ideas that eroded the historical investment in low-cost housing for all in a raid on this sector that helped secure political support while muddying the relationship between the working class and its standard representatives. Right to Buy led to frequent debates about its role in promoting Conservative and property-owning views among even those it was not in their interest to support. Alongside this policy the government also deregulated the mortgage market so that commercial banks could capture the business of mutually owned building societies who were the main lenders to house buyers. The 1986 Building Society Act was passed at a time when publicly owned utilities such as gas, water and telecommunications were also in the process of being privatised.

Over the last two decades government has intensified its critique of public welfare provision, not just council housing but state education, prisons and social services, all of which continue to be castigated as failing services that would benefit from an injection of commercial competition. Problems that were previously attributed to structural processes, such as poverty and inequality, were recast as individual failure so that tenants unable to find secure work were judged responsible for their predicament. These views also extended to the designation of sink estates containing underclasses of residents who were voluntarily detached from work and opportunity. The 'solution' to their problems was often training courses to help individuals in need acquire 'social capital' so as to be better able to compete in the job market even as increasing flexibilisation and outsourcing reduced pay in unskilled jobs. The closure of state and other enterprises in key regions and automation also left a human residuum that was not and could not be incorporated into the labour market.

While local authorities were being denied the necessary funds, the Conservative government introduced measures to support the UK's small but burgeoning housing association sector by aiding associations to build new stock. The associations were not considered to be public sector, so investment in the sector did not generate debt on the public accounts. The 1988 Housing Act created opportunities for local authorities to transfer their stock to housing associations. Between the years 1988 and 2008 as many as half of all local authorities transferred some of their stock (large-scale voluntary transfers).

The late 1990s to 2010s

The election of the Labour government did mitigate some of the maintenance problems within council housing stock but this intervention has been problematic. While the Blair and Brown administrations did invest in public housing through the Decent Homes initiative, the investment in welfare was largely arranged through private finance initiatives which has had a devastating impact on public services by pushing debt costs onto future taxpayers (Raco, 2013). Another feature of the Labour administration's housing policy was the incentives provided to local authorities to divest their stock by establishing arm's-length management organisations. By 2018, 167 out of 326 English local authorities had transferred all their council properties to housing associations (Murie, 2018: 489).

There was some investment in council housing refurbishment through the 'Decent Homes Programme' in 2000, but this was mainly directed to housing stock that was judged to be spaces of social and economic disadvantage. The Labour administration from 1997 to 2010 also relied on the Private Finance Initiative (PFI), initially conceived by the preceding Conservative government, to source housing renewal programmes as well as investment in social infrastructure, such as hospitals and roads. Government debts under this scheme were set over a 30-year period that would ensure that future ratepayers would meet the costs of this loan – the can was again kicked down the road. The PFI was supported by financiers and the banking sector who saw an opportunity to profit from the failings of welfare programmes (Raco, 2013).

The financial crisis of 2008 ultimately served as a justification for public cuts, rather than allowing financial institutions to sink – a choice which has come to decimate UK public services. The austerity programme was predicated on the assumption that attracting financial investment into the UK was a greater priority than welfare expenditure. Speculative housing investment in the UK has increased significantly following the financial crisis, while public housing programmes remain insufficiently funded despite talk (yet again) of such investment being forthcoming. This period has been described as one 'increasing housing marginality and insecurity centred on an expanded private rental sector' (Powell and Robinson, 2019: 193).

With the benefit of hindsight we can see that government increasingly arbitrates between the interests of wealthier property owners and those who lack these resources but who wish to see their fortunes improve. As we explain in the final chapter, one of the reasons policymakers were and are so reluctant to take the necessary steps to address the housing crisis is their fear of an electoral backlash from homeowners and investors who currently benefit from high prices and a shortage of rental housing. There are also commercial interests such as banks whose profits would be reduced should house prices fall significantly in the UK. Housing shortages are a feature of the UK housing system and this can be discerned from Figure 2.3 which charts housing building by each sector from 1946 to 2018. Note the decline of construction rates of local authority house building from the mid-1970s and its only partial substitute by the housing associations from this time. While some estimate the need for 240,000–340,000 new homes a year, we can see that at almost no time have such targets been achieved unless the state was significantly involved in these programmes of construction.

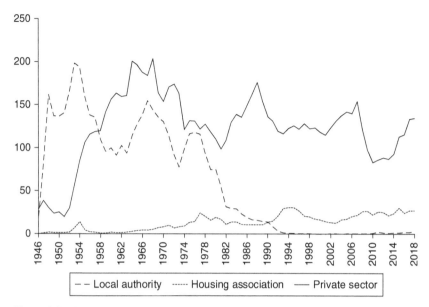

Figure 2.3 Annual completion of UK dwellings 1946–2018

Source: MHCLG Live Table 244

The 2010s–2019

The global financial crisis (GFC) helped provide a justification for a large austerity programme that was the main policy initiative of the UK Conservative–Liberal Democrat coalition that formed the government in 2010. Significant cuts in welfare and housing-related expenditure accelerated the housing problems in the UK, including repairs and maintenance of council properties and social housing building programmes in areas of high demand. Already underfunded, council housing is now available to only the most vulnerable households, yet it must be noted that most of these poor households also work.

The extent of social residualisation in council housing can be shown by contrasting two points in time. In 1962, only 11% of council tenants were deemed economically inactive but by 2003 the percentage of households had reached 65% (Malpass and Victory, 2010). In part, this high figure can be explained by the fact that local authorities had little choice but to prioritise the most disadvantaged households when allocating council tenancies as homes were sold through the Right to Buy. Households who might have been able to access council housing had little option but to rent from private landlords with no security. As many tenants in the private rental market relied on housing benefit to meet their rent, the costs escalated and, in 2017, the average cost of private rental property in England was £210 per week, far higher than the average £88 that is charged by councils and housing associations.

The GFC provided a pretext for governments to extend tax incentives to landlord investors to assist them to 'buy to let'. These policies led to many former council homes being sold to private landlords. Currently, the government pays private landlords £9.3 billion per year in the form of housing benefit and universal credit to accommodate households who would in earlier periods be living in council housing (Turner, 2019). It is also worth looking at what happened to the properties that council tenants bought off councils. Here we can see that in Milton Keynes, for example, as many as 71% of former council properties sold under the Right to Buy legislation were owned by private landlords and many estates in London now not only are privately owned but also see large numbers of properties being sold on to private landlords. It has been estimated by Murie (2016) that the additional cost of accommodating tenants in the private rented sector rather than local authority homes runs to around £800 million per year.

The bad value of privatisation and subsidies to already wealthy owners and landlords have received scant interest from those ostensibly interested in these issues. But the fact that many large landlords now buy up former council housing stock and re-let properties to tenants reliant on rental support without public condemnation can be sourced back to the failure of politicians to take the necessary steps to protect the nation's assets – council housing that had been so time consuming and costly to be built has ended up being sold off cheaply to sitting tenants and new landlords. The net effect of these changes, however, has been to restore and underwrite returns to those who possess the capital of homes to be rented out privately.

The high rents charged by landlords has led to the displacement of many low-income households in some UK inner city areas and the increase of homeless households sleeping rough on the streets. In recent years, there have been cuts to the local housing allowance that low-income renters can access. In practice, these cuts have led to many households being displaced from their neighbourhood. Shelter and other pressure groups have rightly pointed out a connection between these cuts and the rise of homelessness since 2010 with eviction from the private rented sector accounting for the majority of cases.

The low levels of security in the private rented sector have enabled gentrification and related household displacement to accelerate in areas of high demand and competition for housing. Areas of London, such as Hackney and Lambeth, that were traditionally home to working-class households, have changed in ways that would be familiar to residents in locations such as Fulham and Islington in the 1970s. Owner occupiers who move into these neighbourhoods often have considerable wealth and tend to choose private education for their children. Economically, the high costs of housing operate as a brake on consumer spending, as tenants hand over a significant proportion of their earnings to landlords and this proportion is of course higher when incomes are low.

There is some irony in the fact that UK taxpayers substantially subsidise private landlords, mediating these changes via their support through housing benefits and universal credit. In many ways, these processes are the increasingly visible markers of economic differences conferred by housing tenure that interact with income, wealth and identity positions. Here it increasingly seems that landlords and owners are winning out, that property wealth is reproduced through inheritance, and that tenants in both public and private sectors are persistent losers.

Undoubtedly, private landlords have benefitted from government interventions. Anyone walking past the large 'regeneration' schemes in cities like London and Manchester will notice showcase flats intended to entice buyers to purchase a home or a rental investment property. Under the guise of promoting social diversity and improvement, many public housing estates have been opened up to private sector developers to extract profit from the process. Almost without exception, the outcome of renewal has been a loss of public housing which has declined despite local campaigns by tenant activists. It has not been possible to persuade local councils to compel developers to increase the overall number of public housing dwellings following redevelopment. Many developers have managed to convince local authorities that without homes for sale regeneration would not be financially viable and could not proceed. An example is the Aylesbury estate in south London which has resulted in the demolition of 2,000 council homes and a new estate of 3,575 homes that will be completed by 2032. Prior to demolition, the estate was for 2,402 council homes and 356 that were sold under the Right to Buy. The new development will result in 1,323 units for social tenants (managed by Notting Hill Genesis Housing Association), 479 shared ownership and 1,773 for sale (Turner, 2018).

No one would deny the need for repairs and the renewal of many estates. It is necessary and desirable that properties are of a modern and safe standard. Yet under current financial rules, the programmes set up to regenerate estates have been public–private partnerships to ensure that commercial interests gain most from the rise in the value of land and homes. So, public–private partnerships, mixed developments and the initiatives that have been undertaken in a similar form have received support since their benefits accrue beyond the estate itself to nearby homeowners and businesses.

Housing regeneration programmes in the UK provide another salutary reminder that long-term under-investment in public housing is a necessary feature of the current 'housing machine' providing new markets and opportunities for profiteering. Inner London locales such as Bermondsey and Battersea which were traditional working-class districts in the 1970s have changed almost beyond recognition. The collective gains that accrued from the large public sector house building programmes of the 1950–1970s have flowed to wealthier, property-owning households. Should any new large-scale public housing programme one day occur, governments will need to ensure that this time around, their investment is protected from rent seekers and speculators. This outcome seems unlikely.

Conclusion

At the start of this chapter we stated that a systemic understanding of UK housing policy is necessary to make sense of the forces that shape the present housing crisis. We can be clear that, consistently, UK governments have privileged the interest of the wealthy above other social groups, especially since the period from the late 1970s that is often to referred to as 'neoliberal'. Indeed, wealth and class today are heavily shaped by property ownership (or its loss or absence) and by place – the housing system and its operation are fundamental to these forms of inequality and disadvantage. There are other conclusions that can be highlighted. First, the current housing crisis should not be seen as some unfortunate by-product of a 'free market' economy – as some commentators such as Patrick Schumacher (2018) encourage us to believe. In his article for the Adam Smith Institute, he argues that state intervention has distorted the workings of the London housing market, imposing controls on the capacity of developers to build new homes. Only 'denationalisation' and 'depoliticalisation' can resolve the housing crisis according to Schumacher – selling off such assets and privatising yet more public spaces using open markets is the way forward. Such views appear to echo a deep consensus among many today.

A more insightful analysis would be to place stress on the ways that policymakers have yielded to, or work in concert with, the wishes of powerful financial institutions such as banks. It is for this reason that governments have instigated policies that lead to households incurring large debts and forms of investment that privilege speculation. So, for example, the easing of lending restrictions on banks (a feature of the late 1980s) enabled institutions to offer cheap credit to households with insecure income. Households who might have been able to access local authority housing now have had to make do with renting in an unstable and poor-quality private sector, or have borrowed large sums to purchase a home with the attendant risks of mortgage default.

Our second conclusion is that, aside from the obvious damage and pain inflicted on some of the poorest households, there have been other notable impacts of these policy decisions. The first and most obvious of these has been that the UK has become an even more divided nation, both in terms of household wealth (a much more important measure of inequality than just annual income) and spatially. Many of the poorest communities now reside on the suburban outskirts of the largest cities and many of the former industrialised towns in the north of England and South Wales have difficulties in attracting investment to secure stable job opportunities. Meanwhile, investment and attention flow to already hot property markets, notably the south-east. Other factors have also been significant. For example, developments in digital technologies have disrupted traditional employment configurations. What is frequently referred to as the opportunities of a 'gig' economy conceals how many workers are required to act as self-employees and endure insecurity and low wages. These forms of precarity interact with the housing system to reveal often hyper-mobile, insecure and intensely unhappy groups who navigate a costly and inadequate housing system.

Finally, the 1980s have arguably had the most enduring legacy. The combination of monetarist fiscal policies imposed by the Conservative government and the deregulation of the finance and banking sector through legislation, such as the Building Society Act 1986, Social Security Act 1986 and Financial Services Act 1986, created the opportunities for privatisation of the UK's welfare state, including that of housing. This was effectively the start of what is now commonly referred to as a period of neoliberalism, in which government policymakers sought to promote privatisation and welfare cuts as a necessary corrective to improve the competitiveness of the UK economy. As scholars have explained, government policies have simultaneously sought to cut the cost of public services and support while developing practices that privilege the private sector and capital over and above collective provision. Much of today's crisis is linked to these interventions.

Notes

1. Engels was not alone in deeply criticising landlords. David Ricardo and Adam Smith made significant critiques of those who produced nothing and who controlled and extracted incomes by renting out land or property.
2. These economic incentives have been further implanted in social life via the expansion of 'property porn' television programming; the widespread interest in making money from the purchase, renovation and sale of homes; and playing the market to make a profit.

what do we know?

Introduction

One of the things we frequently encounter in relation to the housing situation today is the impression that if we could just increase the supply of housing then most problems would be ameliorated. Affordability and access to a decent home would be within greater reach. Intuitively many of us know this. But why do we know this issue so well? How have these particular messages filtered through so clearly? What many media stories and experts dwell on is the blockages that appear to get in the way of more efficient housing development and these are usually pinned on an inefficient state bureaucracy in the form of local authority planners and an overly tight regulation of land supply. Questions of the quality, the disproportionate power wielded by banks, developers and real estate agencies, regional and urban location, and tenure of housing tend to be dismissed in these analyses. There is a crisis right now, so we simply need more housing.

Consider, for example, the judgement of Boris Johnson in a speech he gave at the Conservative Party Conference in October 2018:

> It is a disgraceful fact that we now have lower rates of owner occupation – for under-40s – than the French or the Germans. That reflects the failure of governments for the last 30 years to build enough housing. But it is also a massive opportunity for us Tories. (Johnson, 2018)

We need to reflect on how such a diagnosis undermines efforts to advance the case for affordable housing in the UK today. One of the clearest effects of framing the debate in this way is that it enables developers to present themselves as being aligned with the desires of low- and modest-income households. It also makes it easier for them to apply pressure on central and local governments to build what they want, where they want and to the standards that they decide. While this pressure by no means wins out in all cases, it does generate a high demand and lobbying activity to achieve the kind of market conditions that will promote the profit expectations of the development industries and property machine more broadly.

We will argue that it is increasingly the case that pressure to build on preferable terms has benefitted developers to the detriment of most people. Worse, the system, as it operates, combines the interests of capital, profit and political gaming over and above the needs of everyday households. In crude terms, what we have is a system that is broken but the source of this malfunction is frequently misdiagnosed (even governments whose interests are aligned with the property sector will often *appear* to acknowledge this).

We will often hear that the housing system is not working for capital which seeks the support of government and access to open land and a large cohort of buyers who can then purchase homes and property. The lack of good-quality and affordable housing, we are often told, is due to a series of impediments that prevent the market from operating efficiently. Despite this, we also know that holding on to land (land banking) and leaving it undeveloped is an important means of raising profit rates. In 2018, a report in *The Times* showed that of 1.7 million planning applications by builders granted between 2006 and 2014, less than half had been completed after three years. So here we note these issues to flag how the combined interests of development, finance and politics are necessarily ranged against the needs of most people seeking to buy homes for their own use.

We will set out in this chapter an analysis of the housing system and its various key components alongside a perspective of its operation that helps us to disentangle some of the complex roots generating the apparent crisis 'above ground' that we all see. Our argument, put simply, is that public attention is often misdirected by the alluring idea that the chief impediments to enough good housing lie in the inefficient work of planning departments, planning regulations or the cost and availability of land, and that these factors need to be deregulated or subsidised to achieve the desired result – more and cheaper homes for all. Yet what happens, if we look into the operation of the housing system, its key institutions, actors and its history, is that these same problems have been identified recurrently for more than a hundred years.

More than a century ago the question was presented in terms of how it was that, despite a strong incentive to privately produce abundant housing to profit from the massive demand, neither the state nor private developers looked to resolve these conditions. The answer to that question established that speculative developers *required* a shortage of housing stock to extract greater profit for capital. So, slum conditions, overcrowding and badly built housing can be understood as a built-in method by which profits could be maximised by an industry that responds purely in relation to economic, rather than social, motives. As we will see, there remain strong continuities with that time because the underlying structures and the privileging of speculative forms of capital continue to enable investment in land speculation rather than productive activities to resolve the crisis in housing.

We can think of the housing question today as still being essentially about how people in a given society can be adequately, happily and securely housed. We can extend this question to a concern with the way in which the private home, as a critical anchor point in everyone's lives, should operate to enable human capacities and potential. Notably such a question is not and should not be conceived as one of how the home can be used as a means of making money or the source of private or corporate wealth (often termed exchange value). In a very important sense, we might say that homes are too important for that because the use of a home is central to human life. But, as we will see, an enormous circuit of profitable and increasingly central economic activity is devoted to the construction, trade and financing of homes that is judged critical to the health of the national economy. This centrality, the key role that housing plays economically, is also linked to land and financial services that operate in a capitalist economy. Of course, these operations are also subject to interaction with, and regulation by, the political formations that constitute government and this generates outcomes which, while sticking to an agenda of seeing housing as a vehicle for profit making, vary over time. To take one example of this, we might look at how a capitalist economy like the UK's has periodically engaged in the construction of homes by the state (council housing) or the regulation of private rents.

The main result of acknowledging these deep and powerful imperatives and invested interests, the logic of this system if you will, is that we
can identify the housing system as consisting of two key components. In
this system there lies a cluster of institutions and interests framed around
the economic and political uses and advantages that come from housing
(the property machine), on the one hand, and the everyday social uses and
users wrapped up in core human needs as the second component (the
social machine). Critically, we need to understand that these two components are in significant tension with each other, the latter offering a brake
or a partial steer on the former. Even more crucially, we must understand
that these two components operate from very unequal positions of power
and influence! But once we have this basic understanding, we can begin
to think more clearly about who is being incentivised to do what and how
the resulting property machine operates without interest or commitment to
social outcomes. These results include what many now identify as badly
built homes that are purchased at high cost, often in which unhappy buyers
are locked into long-term financial indebtedness (mortgages) but who yet
frequently count themselves as lucky to start on some ladder of personal
wealth accumulation. In this sense, much seems to be wrong.

These perverse outcomes are often defended in media stories and
pushed by developers and the property industry more broadly. Our economy
offers particular incentives to key actors seeking profits (banks and often
indeed many homeowners) from housing, as well as those who benefit from a
privately profitable property economy (investment funds, banks, financiers,
pension funds and indeed political actors and groups). The housing system is
dominated by these sectors and powerful interests. But this is where things
get more interesting because this is now a much more complex story than
one of big bad capital versus the goodly working population. The property
machine is a much more enveloping, diffuse and complex reality into which
very many of us in some way fit, benefit or even require its operation in order
to generate well-being from it. In reality, many people and households are
conscripted into this system and become its unconscious or active defenders.
This is because we may be homeowners seeking to buy low and sell high
(looking for an up and coming area); we may be tenants wanting to stop
wasting money on rent and to buy our own place, while some owners may be
landlords who have bought a property to accumulate capital for their retirement; in other cases we will find pensioners whose weekly income partly
results from property investments made on their behalf, and so on.

The logic of property and housing is that profit and capital are part of the stuff of everyday life and that their operation underpins a much deeper embedding of pro-market assumptions that then filter into and infect our culture and the operation of our politics. Somehow, we all appear to 'know' that rising house prices, increased house building, low interest rates and homeownership are indicators of a good, improving or stable economy. A profitable trade in homes is not only a good thing but also the most efficient way to manage the economy. That homes are bought and sold is how things *are*. This sense of the primacy of profit and private property relations has become so normalised that it can be difficult to take stock, stand back and ask: how is it that I appear to know what I know? Why do I desire a particular trajectory through my life in relation to the housing I wish to buy, sell and live in? Who or what shapes this system, its parameters and incentives in ways that affect my life so deeply? Perhaps more importantly, we might finally ask: how do these tacitly held beliefs actually come to foreclose and effectively occlude other, competing ideas about how we might address human housing need more effectively than we currently do?

It is no overstatement to observe that how we live is fundamentally connected to the home we have access to, the place we live in. But look around for a moment and consider the intense variety of human experience as it is shaped by varying national housing systems. Housing is about much more than questions of supply and demand which, to take one example, have the effect of sometimes suggesting that how we live is a question simply of market economics – more supply somehow means we all get to be happy householders as prices are kept down. If we somehow get the numbers right all will be well, we will all have a home and prices will be set at a reasonable rate.

As we have already stated, the prevailing view of markets in homes as the best possible system of allocation and benefit is upheld in media conversations and political life. But such a view sidesteps two important issues. First, those developing housing privately and investing in it have an absolute interest in not resolving the supply question because to do so erodes their returns. Second, there are much deeper sets of class interests and powerful institutional actors (political and corporate) built into the housing system. These interests inevitably seek to influence and call for the housing system to be managed in such a way that helps expand their personal wealth (such as the desire for low interest rates and low personal tax rates) and to be enabled to 'reproduce' personal wealth through housing inheritance (by keeping inheritance taxes low). In a crude sense this framing of housing issues purposefully aligns the interests of capital and property on the one hand with social needs, consumers and the bulk of the working population on the other.

An insightful framing of these issues would recognise that while these interests overlap at times, it is capital that is ultimately the winner. These framings of housing can be discussed, but they must not be ignored if we are to reach a more nuanced account of what we know about the housing system we live in and how we might begin to improve it. We must recognise how it is that finance capital has a trajectory akin to an impersonal and powerful force – it seeks to expand and grow and these qualities also mean that it has no particular interest in tenure, rights and housing quality unless these issues are linked to the deeper question of profits.

Capital is deeply interrelated with the field and regulatory actions of the state. Neither the housing system nor the economy are abstract entities 'out there', rather they are entwined in complex ways. This makes the need to rein in and put these forces in service of human need, something that is eminently possible. Yet the profit imperative that underpins societies with strong market orientations will always tend to flow into new spaces and to provide new expanding opportunities for investment. As we write, US finance capital is being invested in public, non-profit housing in the UK and Europe while swathes of new tower blocks are being built to lure wealthy foreign investors in London, for example. In this sense, we need to recognise the need for more progressive state action that arbitrates more fully in favour of consumers and citizens and while orchestrating and regulating capital in ways that might help to achieve these outcomes.

Capital is frequently abetted and underwritten by government – indeed, what we call capitalism is itself shaped by the relationship between corporate, commercial and investment actors and the political domain which retains significant powers. Such a conceptualisation may be attacked as being a cynical, leftist or a kind of 'radical' analysis. But think what is happening when governments extend quantitative easing, Help to Buy, the unhousing of people through estate demolitions, the extension of profit motives to the running of public housing, the compulsion to sell housing association properties and council housing, among other examples of state actions to pave the way for capital.

The UK is in many ways a nation in which housing has become almost fully an asset without reference to the satisfaction of basic human need. Today, the role of capital at the heart of this model is becoming more clearly apparent as political economists highlight its operation – housing is increasingly an asset to be milked by investors and owners and the dividend of these operations flows back to a limited number of key actors. The role of the state, particularly in the past decade, has become one of signalling new opportunities for capital while allowing poorer and excluded households to be pushed from one tenancy to another, or to be made homeless by changes in work opportunities and welfare changes. This may seem a bold assertion, so let us add some flesh to the bones of our argument!

Inequality is a critical element of today's housing question. The consumption of housing is an important element of how such inequalities are reproducing and worsening these outcomes. Owning land, property or a home places one within the system of accumulation and capital itself. This fact in many ways makes conscripts of homeowners to the logic of a property machine more generally. Here we might think of the way in which buying a home is described as getting onto a ladder. In fact, this is a powerful metaphor used to suggest we are moving 'up' – once here one can begin to grow and expand personal wealth (though of course it is not without risks).

But what of the households not on these wealth escalators? Half of England is owned by less than 1% of the population; in terms of personal wealth the richest 10% of households hold 44% of all wealth. The top 10% of households by income own on average property worth £300,000, while the bottom 30% of households own nothing at all (ONS Wealth and Assets Survey, 2018). Homeownership helps to reproduce these inequalities as housing wealth is a key element of inheritance. One may also make the important point that access to homeownership has helped to build real wealth for many, though these gains have gone into reverse in recent years as the numbers of (particularly younger) homeowners have declined enormously.

Without effective or fairer wealth, inheritance and land taxes we can see how these loops of wealth and disadvantage are reproduced intergenerationally and how they tend to expand over people's lives. Someone who bought a UK home in 1980 for £50,000 would in 2019 see that investment having risen almost tenfold in value (to £476,000). A private or public tenant over this period would simply have given up a chunk of their income with nothing to show for it, though the public tenant would have been more securely and cheaply housed. In reality, these choices and apparent losses require closer scrutiny – it is not so much that the tenant has lost money but a question of the relative compulsion to become a tenant in the face of local housing options and household income. Someone on a low income renting a good-quality publicly managed home (and of course not all public homes achieve this standard) with security of tenure is in a very different position to someone else in a bedsit padding the pension of a landlord and enduring bad conditions. But to return to the wealth question we can see how, given the current legislative and housing landscape we occupy, it is better to own and indeed to be the offspring of an owner who will also likely inherit a lump sum at some point.

What these general points move us towards is the need to locate and analyse the kind of underlying system of interests and forces that are often hard to understand at first sight. We need to get to grips with this system, to prise open its operation and examine some of its working components. On one level, what we are of course looking at here are the fundamental features of a capitalist economy, which operates within and across national boundaries. There is a need to widen our focus to one that takes in global interests and processes – pension funds, financiers, investors, investment vehicles as emissaries of capital that are looking to make gains from a menu of possible investment locations around the world. One of the results of these flows of money is the entwinement of the property machine in distinctive political arrangements that see the management of the economy, and housing's key role in that economy (given its relationship to the work of builders, developers, banks, building suppliers, and so on), as a key part of its everyday work.

A key effect of the entwinement of capital with politics is a kind of lockstep arrangement in which governments come to view their role as being one of promoting and assisting capital and investment interests since these are understood as the basis of sound management of the national economy. For capital, its interests are best secured by working with government and to seek forms of financial, planning and building regulation and economic management that help to de-risk their investments and to maintain maximum returns. What we will notice is that concern with house buyers, the homeless, the overcrowded and the poor do not feature much in these arrangements, except insofar as any of these groups may be encouraged or compelled to sign up to finance arrangements to help them pay for their housing, which is another major source of profit by banks and other lenders.

It is important to understand the interests that are a feature of the property machine, on the one hand, and those of the bulk of house-holds who are not wealthy, and who are often managed, contained, curtailed and indeed damaged by elite political and economic interests, on the other. Housing has increasingly become a key domain for political-economic action that is increasingly detached from a concern with those who are locked out or who have little. A major role for politics and policy becomes one of stage managing a system that inflates the role and return of housing as a financial asset, given the kind of personal wealth and benefits that return to homeowners, banks, builders and other key insti-tutions involved in the speculation and investment in housing, such as pension companies and hedge funds. In a very crude sense, if these arrangements can be managed effectively, the real prize is electoral success as a sufficiently large enough constituency of interests and voters align themselves with or indeed are enrolled into desiring these outcomes (in terms of financial rewards to those involved as actors and institutions within the property machine). So, while we may focus on issues such as housing supply, to take one example, the govern-ment's professed interest in this problem belies a primary concern with maintaining and driving the machine. The state will tend to act in the interests of powerful actors and institutions who are aligned with the property machine as a whole.

Many will say that there are not enough homes; even prominent Conservative Party politicians pronounce that the housing system is 'broken'. Consider the remarks of Jacob Rees-Mogg who wrote in 2019 that 'the state of housebuilding is "more catastrophe than crisis", with the UK scarred by "identikit estates", "nimbyism", and under the charge of "big housebuilding corporations"' (Rees-Mogg and Tylecote, 2019; quoted by Collinson, 2019). Such remarks are telling because they invoke notions of a response (new, ugly and intrusive housing) that is worrisome for many communities who tend to prevent new development. These are certainly issues and it is important to understand how many promoting housing supply disingenuously skirt around the complexities of getting permission and construction in play in particular areas.

It is often remarked that housing is too expensive and that those seeking opportunities are being locked out. Record levels of homeownership, the use of temporary accommodation, housing benefit to those in need and unstable households buffeted around the system are evident features and indicators of a lack of housing. Yet at the same time as we see this crisis played out, we have seen record levels of profitability among the major housebuilders, record-breaking dividends to the owners and managers of these corporations, and rising house prices. We have also seen a massive expansion in Buy to Let mortgages for affluent individual landlords (one in ten homes are sold to landlords), the creation of hundreds of tower blocks sold as investments to offshore investors, the entry of predatory investment companies into public housing and a massive expansion of intensely profitable construction in cities like London for the rich who themselves have grown rapidly in number over the same decade or so. What is going on? Certainly, it seems increasingly possible to make a link between the apparent vitality of property and capital and a set of pernicious housing outcomes. The links between these disparities is complex and nested within a longer history of privilege and political inaction that has always tended to accede to the demands of capital.

We will start our analysis with the *property machine* before moving to consider the *social domain* of interests and outcomes which many now view as being subordinate to the machine's needs. But we also need to acknowledge that the social domain has an often contradictory or antagonistic relationship to the property machine because, in many ways, it is enrolled into a system whose material rewards are desired by many, even as these rewards are signs of forms of alienation and oppression for many others – the machine delivers big winners and arguably even bigger losers, but this does not pause many in their pursuit of housing wealth.

Much politicking and housing policy action has its limits largely set by the interests of capital to maintain a stable system in which profit rates, accumulation (often through the dispossession of vulnerable households) and withdrawal from costly social markets (public housing) render outcomes for many households pretty desperate. This context generates important consequences for how we might imagine, or re-imagine, action around housing questions and crises. In other words, that something deeper and more 'radical' is required if everyone is to be properly housed in ways that allow them to lead a dignified and thriving life. Capital will not relinquish its demands without a fight – indeed, its interests are so embedded in the operation of the system that it does not need to. Of course, we can see the need that households should be helped (by governments and by lenders) to lead a prosperous life but such prosperity is defined sectionally by tenure (owners) and in terms of wealth rather than seeing access to a good home as a form of prosperity in its own right that all should be allowed to achieve.

In the operation of a system hardwired in this way it tends to yield only deeper social gaps and class divisions as it generates winners and losers. Worse still, such a system in reality is set to operate in such a way that its winners tend to keep on winning, those with wealth can buy more, investors can expand portfolios of property holdings, and inheritance enables the rich to start life with enormous advantages that can be used to build further wealth. To provide for those on low incomes only represents an encumbrance on these ambitions. This ability for those with capital to build greater wealth far outstrips the capacity of others without it to earn and save their way to some kind of wealth.[1]

The property machine

Here we will try to describe the important constellations of interests, actors and institutions that have been called the property machine (Ambrose and Colenutt, 1975). This machine is closely tied to and entwined with the workings and imperatives of the capitalist system itself. Far from being a system devoted to a capitalist class that is the owner of factories and the production of commodities, the capitalist system we inhabit today is one increasingly linked to finance which itself operates as an important set of loops and circuits that also help to expand capital.

Capital itself is the defining feature of economies like that of the UK which is one nation among many in a more or less global system of capitalist economies. Capital is essentially money in motion, moving through investments so that it can expand still further. This growth imperative is the hallmark of what can be described as a capitalist economy – without growth it appears to wither. Importantly, governments in capitalist economies are compelled to understand their role as overseeing, co-ordinating and ushering around capital formations in ways that allow the key institutions of those societies, the wealthy and middle classes, to benefit.

It is hard to find a better example of these processes of capital in motion than the market in housing. Yet the idea of the market itself is also highly problematic. The metaphor of a market suggests buyers and vendors acting with relative freedom. Yet the reality is that the housing market in particular is formed of massively unequal positions between the enormous vested interests of capital, and it is heavily rigged in ways that help to bring returns to capital over and above the needs and interests of those who are often described as consumers. The housing market operates in a social system that is already riven by class, gendered, regional, ethnic and other inequalities that are highly relevant to forms of well-being and wealth.

At this point it is helpful to make a distinction between capitalism and markets since markets, often seen as the hallmark of systems such as ours, can also be found in many non- or pre-capitalist societies. This is an important point of difference because of course many critics of those advancing ideas that might challenge or redirect market provision are often not interested in the abolition of market provision, but rather seek to curtail and manage the excesses of capital and its inadequate resolution of housing need.

To return to the key issue at stake, housing increasingly provides the means by which capital can be put into play and expanded through various forms of investment, such as the speculative purchase and sale of homes (which may involve homeowners or institutional players and investors), the acquisition of land, construction and sale of homes or in a return to capitalists via rents on land and homes. The apparent magic of such a system lies in the way that incentives, prices and actors combine in ways that appear to deliver not just homes but an expanding sense of wealth (though one that is selectively realised among particular social groups) that can also then be used to help fund the more tangible purchase of lifestyle goods and opportunities by those benefitting from these gains.

We support the analogy of a property machine to foreground the constellation of continuing interests, incentives, actors and institutions that circulate around the question of how to generate profits and wealth from the construction, maintenance, investment in and management of housing. But as we will see, it is the capacity of this circuit to appear to offer the realisation of dreams and well-being to a sufficiently large section of a society that allows its legitimacy to continue without significant challenges.

Many among those who rent, to take one example, might see little to be gained from challenging the ways that this system produces winners and losers (among whom they often count themselves) to produce a fairer system. Rather, many renters may identify themselves as hopefuls waiting to buy and may be very happy to take advantage of assistance to become part of that group through government schemes like Save to Buy schemes or subsidies for new owners. If only they could be helped to buy, they would be on the ladder!

The ideological hold of homeownership is powerful. The example of renters waiting to become owners helps to illustrate the capacity of the system to align many who might otherwise be critical of its deficiencies – conscripting many who cannot identify viable or clear alternatives but who may be seduced by its offer of a place of one's own and perhaps a pot of cash at the point of sale. In this sense, many for whom the system does *not* and *will* not work still submit to it in the hope that they too can enlarge in some sense their own portfolio and embark on a project that so many share in which ownership of a home is seen to confer wealth, well-being, a refuge and place of reduced costs to maintain during a period of retirement before death. In this sense they want more of such a system, not less of it.

Criticism of homeownership should nevertheless be carefully presented. In light of poor standards in rented housing, high costs and the potential intrusion of landlords into the lives and matters of tenants, owning one's home has much to commend it. And, in so many ways, given these structures and rules of the system as they stand, these outcomes are truths that can be recognised and easily understood by many – the way things work does indeed seem to deliver to many. Who wishes to pay rent over their lifetime? Who would not want an appreciating asset that could be used to help purchase big-ticket items including holidays of a finite lifetime, cars, or even privately supplied education to help our offspring pursue some advantages when they come to an increasingly precarious labour market?

But to return again to the analogy of the machine, the point here is that we need to understand the various constituent groups of a capitalist orientation to investment and growth to see how this brings sectional interests and particular incentives. Within this machine we find the banks, who offer the finance which underwrites the system as a whole, offering loans to developers alongside other investors, mortgages to consumers seeking to buy homes on increasingly liberal terms in order to help the value of assets rise.

The second key group here is the developers and builders who speculatively seek land or other development opportunities. Most of the builders in the UK are very large, the top 10% of builders building nearly half (47%) of homes. This is an intensely, and increasingly, profitable sector in large part because of its ability to control large landholdings and to offer a controlled supply of new homes in order to maintain profit rates – a few homes are put on sale at a time in order to control the illusion that there are only ever 'Just a few remaining!'.

The third key part of the machine is the state itself, both government and its role in planning for development. Here the state performs a critical intervention by co-ordinating, regulating and managing the macroeconomy in ways that protect the operations overseen by finance and development. These interventions come in the form of interest rate setting (delegated to the Bank of England), legislating to intervene in housing provision (deciding on whether to build public or social housing, subsidies or taxes for owners, landlords, builders) and setting rules for planning and development that shape the overall set of signals that developers then respond to.

Over the past 40 years the state has become less and less interested in being responsible for the direct provision and management of (council) housing. Despite massive failures by market providers to accommodate poorer households, the state has proclaimed that private provision and ownership are preferred models of providing housing. It is clear that the pursuit of these private goals has undermined greater access to home-ownership as prices have risen and cash-rich older generations and private investors have bought private and indeed public housing – in many cases then renting it to younger and lower income households!

What therefore needs to be understood clearly is that the state acts as a key intermediary for the interests of the financial and development sectors. So, while it is true that financial institutions have found clever ways to integrate and expand their role in numerous areas of social and economic life, they have also benefitted from the key signals and efforts of government that have espoused a pro-development and pro-ownership regime. This is not the same, note, as claiming that government is keen on increasing supply, but rather that it seeks to enable a stable and profitable operating environment for the property machine as a whole. Often these ambitions are wrapped up in macroeconomic objectives in which rising house prices, construction activity and sales become major indicators of economic activity.

The state is also part of this property machine since it not only is connected to these interests but also benefits in its electoral ambitions by frequently seeking to be understood as speaking for the interests of existing and prospective homeowners – in many cases fudging the issue that these two groups are in many ways antagonistic to each other since to lower prices to help the latter will aggravate the former! So it is a difficult ambition indeed given that it requires government to appear to embrace the interests of both constituencies – stating that it wishes to see the wealth of housing asset holders appreciate (a property-owning democracy as some have called it) and also that it wishes to see access improve by new entrants to homes that are increasingly expensive and which require significant support that is then expressed as even higher house prices. In reality, much of what goes on takes the form of directly empowering and benefitting existing owners of capital and offering, on the other hand, the more or less illusory dream of access to homeownership among those who may never attain it. Yet this dream remains just enough to galvanise political support, the sense that something will be done (but, ultimately, never is).

Partly to appease existing homeowners, many of the government's economic policies are aligned with the Bank of England's decision to lower interest rates to encourage new entrants to the housing market to borrow money. In order to keep an increasingly expensive market moving, efforts need to be made to reduce the cost of borrowing and entry as far as possible. This is why the monthly decisions of the committee that decides these interest rate movements is so closely watched because it is widely understood that they will have massive consequences for the national economy as it revolves around the construction and sale of housing. The participation of new entrants is ultimately essential to ensure that house prices and profits from owning a home will increase over time.

At this point we should also note that for around the past 40 years the political stripe of the party in power has not mattered a great deal and that declining public subsidies, forms of deregulation and direct subsidies to capital have increasingly been evident (such as through sales of public housing, dwindling public investment in housing, and imputed subsidies to developers and investors). This highlights a further important point:

governments within a capitalist economy will tend to coalesce around similar points of action and intervention despite their apparent ideological differences.

For renters and those on low incomes, government will tend to present itself as a champion of increased supply and a facilitator of mechanisms to further cement a 'property-owning democracy'. Of course, balancing these aspirations is very difficult and so governments have tended to try to appease both homeowners and renters with continuous talk of expanding supply in the future – macroeconomic measures to create an environment that allows house prices to remain stable or to increase, and so on.

The property machine can be imagined as a combination of broadly aligned interests, to some extent in tension but more or less all assigned to the task of augmenting capital – the stuff accruing to the winners of this system (homeowners, landlords, politicians, financiers, investors) who may see the foundation of their wealth protected. This means that proposals for a stronger government role in public housing provision are often framed as a threat.

Of course, this has not always been so and we need to remember that in the 1950s and 1960s, when the power relationship between labour and capital had shifted to become more conciliatory, the state also sought to mediate conflicts – underwriting markets by offering forms of subsidy, regulation and support to wage earners and more excluded groups. In this period, it was recognised that it was in the interests of capital to ensure that there was demand in the system and that political dissent would not provide a challenge to the legitimacy of the system and the winners within it.

For perhaps the last 20 years or so, this kind of system has changed; it has found new ways to 'emancipate', deregulate and free labour from various forms of support while allowing private markets and credit systems to fill these gaps. Those on low incomes are offered mortgages on increasingly lengthy terms, for example. Largely, this has occurred without popular forms of criticism or mobilised action because in many ways the machine has appeared to deliver for the majority. This apparently unpalatable conclusion is often not faced sufficiently by those advocating a stronger direct government provision of housing. But there are reasons perhaps to think that such a system and the dominance of the property machine have reached certain limits and will see renewed challenges, as we will show in the next chapter.

We use the word 'crisis' with some reservation as it risks conveying that what is happening is some temporary phenomenon that will eventually return to a market equilibrium. In reality, periodic forms of housing crisis, notably sudden collapses in house prices, have proved to be beneficial to capitalism. Drops in house prices act as a break on risk-averse home-owners while enabling those with cash to buy these assets up cheaply, as was seen after the last major crisis when massive investment companies bought homes at effectively sale prices to rent or sell later on.

Crisis is a feature in our heavily finance-oriented context and it is evident that the promotion of homeownership is secondary to the support for ownership by capital wielded by banks and investment companies (including pension funds). The period of what many describe as finan-cialisaton is one in which homes are treated as assets and assembled as portfolios of holdings that offer income returns from rents that can also be sold on as forms of financial products. The other beneficiaries here are landlords and, to a lesser extent, existing and prospective owners whose mortgage debts prop up and maintain revenue for capital.[2] All of this facilitates a spiral of indebtedness and the contradiction at the heart of housing policy. On the one hand, such policy seeks to manage and help citizens, but on the other hand it demonstrably maintains the revenue streams to ensure the conjunction of capital forces are able to profit from the housing crisis.

The social domain

Now we move to the second feature of the housing system, what we call here the social domain. This is the constellation of interests, experiences and actors who use and need homes to ensure their own development and security – every working household in fact. Our analysis of the social domain highlights the centrality of the home to the life of the household, including its flourishing, inclusion, achievement and the realisation of human potential.

In contrast to the systemic features of the property machine, the social machine may appear secondary and less important. This is because the triumph of economic thinking is that it has tended to invade and occupy questions of social life, subordinating them as secondary when, in reality, so much of how we live is dependent on the political and economic management of the societies we live in. These are big issues and raise a set of further questions not only about how we live today but also the way we construct our identities. Our purpose in this section is to provide an analysis of how the property machine has shifted our understanding of our social and domestic life to become one that is much more embedded in the logic of profit and the sense of the social self as something attached to notions of material gain that can be realised through the pursuit of housing wealth.

To put our aims more plainly, we suggest that the housing economy and the political messages we see around us have generated an impression of the home as a place of wealth creation and profiting, rather than celebrating and realising its role as a place to be used, experienced and cherished as the place from which so much of the rest of our experience of life emanates.

The home is necessary for our everyday functioning, but this feature is distorted by governments and financial institutions who encourage us to see our homes primarily as an asset, rather than as a social good. This expectation is easily reinforced because, as we have already suggested, many people are fully signed up and seek to exploit the possibility of using their home, or the purchase of other houses, as a means to make money. In an uncertain world, in which questions about who will provide work or the realisation of a decent income in retirement (the state's diminishing offer of a pension further amplifies this function of housing), this role of housing as a source of speculative gain has in many ways triumphed. It is supported and whipped up by a wider cultural narrative in which ownership and investment are spoken of and strategised by some 'property porn' programmes on TV and in columns in the financial press and elsewhere.

The question becomes how to get more, how to get ahead and how to win within a competitive system. It would be inappropriate and even erroneous to offer a pathological interpretation of individuals whose lives are entangled in the property ownership, investment and wealth nexus. But we can, nevertheless, see how these phenomena are symptomatic of an increasingly cultural and psychological attachment to a system that is by turns impacting negatively on the well-being of a growing number of households.

Where we live and whether we own or rent (from a housing association or a private landlord) are just the beginning of a much longer story about where we go in our lives and how we experience that life. Homes are connected and valued in relation to access to work and educational opportunities, the home shapes our physical and mental health, and it protects us or brings us into contact with risks like crime or environmental problems (such as flooding or pollution). In this sense, housing and our home are the core of our social existence. In many ways these aspects of our domestic lives are so taken for granted that their value is diminished in the face of the more economistic understanding of the home.

As we have already suggested, the property machine bypasses questions concerning social well-being. Homes are designed without space for furniture to maximise profits, borrowers are mis-sold mortgages, estates are developed without greenspace, rents are set at levels that make a social life challenging at best. These realties should not be viewed as market failure but instead as a necessary component of the operation of property machineries created and maintained in order to extract maximum value and profit. These mechanisms of extraction include land deals, home sales, rents and complex financial instruments to investors of various kinds, including pension companies seeking benefits for their members. The result of all of this is the underscoring and increasing inequalities we see around us, many of which are fuelled by those able to participate or not in an increasingly property-oriented economy.

Much of what really counts in the everyday life of households gets caught up in the froth of political statements, media discussions and punterism more broadly that tries to identify the superficial roots of the housing crisis. This is the point at which discussions of how to build and borrow more and how to 'win' in property investment shine through, as does debate about questions of greenfield land and how to build more. But to say these are frothy issues of course is in no way intended to detract from the pain and suffering that we now see around us – record homelessness; encampments in the streets by the homeless (which are then cleared or designed out); young children moving regularly between temporary accommodation that damages their education; the perversely high cost to the state of housing benefit which goes to private landlords seeking profits, often via tenants living in former council houses sold at a discount under Right to Buy (Greater London Assembly, 2018); and so on.

There is really a world of pain out there in which many households suffer conditions of homelessness; the loss of control over their lives (such as that experienced by those living in temporary accommodation); and those living in overcrowded or ill-served by rabbit hutch homes built by massively profitable developers whose consumers are lent to by banks who do not care about these questions of design, appropriateness or environmental sustainability. In such a world, the idea of a housing ladder or a housing career is a kind of cruel illusion, instead a world of exclusion from opportunity which has been worsened by welfare reforms – bedroom tax; stripping of housing benefit from young people; the erosion of homelessness services, among others. All of these issues further interact with changes in the world of work which is now more precarious and which makes sustaining a home more difficult or alternatively a more worrisome process of survival.

The final key point to restate here is that the housing crisis is best understood in a multidimensional way. At one level we can see how it is connected to questions of supply but also how the property machine has defined and controlled the terms on which such questions are resolved. For the social machine, the role of capital represents a kind of answer that is popularly invoked even as we increasingly realise that the resolution of housing problems will only ever be partial. The possibility that some winnings or gain can be taken by the individual household has increasingly driven a culture of speculation within everyday life in which the idea of buying and selling even one's own home for personal gain is identified as some kind of triumph.

Through the examples we have offered here we are able to see how complex and embracing the logic of money and capital is to shaping our ideas about how we might identify effective solutions. Much of the social domain, though antagonised and let down by capital, either remains dependent on it or seeks entry to its rewards. Most such solutions tend to be constructed from key interests and groups taken from the very development and finance sectors whose primary interest is in profitability. What this reveals is a significant contest and tension between the interests and actions of a powerful property machine and the much weaker, fragmented and in many ways co-opted or partially enrolled membership of everyday households into its operation.

Conclusion

In this chapter we have put forward a framework for understanding housing issues in the UK, which is a necessary start if these problems are to be addressed through political or concerted forms of action. What we have highlighted is how the interests and structures that underlie the system we operate within tend to move away from such concerted action precisely because to do so would undermine the need for capital to expand and for the fortunes of the minority to be challenged. This is not intended as a cynical or conspiratorial observation, but instead is based on advanced research in political, economic, planning, finance, law, sociological and geographical assessments of our contemporary housing crisis. This work increasingly highlights the tensions between the requirement of capital for expansion and the social needs of the bulk of households who require stable, affordable, decent homes that serve their long-term human needs for flourishing in secure contexts.

We have tried to show how it is that such a system, which in many ways produces the problems it ostensibly appears to wish to resolve, generates forms of social being that conscript and buy in many whose interests are not best served by it. Many renters, pensioners and vulnerable households seek entry to the world of homeownership, and hope someday to be on the 'ladder' of opportunity and personal wealth that ownership confers. The reality is that the system as it is currently assembled can never deliver for a large number of people who must by necessity be 'failed' in order that profit rates are maintained for banks and builders, and that the political system benefits by appearing to arbitrate and take an active interest in the plight of renters, the homeless, and so on (who are also then failed). Armed with an impression, a mind's-eye view of the clusters of interests and the tendency to crisis from which capital itself feeds and expands, how do we begin to move forward? That is the focus of our next chapter.

Notes

1. This point is made using massive runs of historical data by Piketty (2014) who showed that in capitalist economies the return to capital is always far greater than the increase in wealth that those earning their money from wages can ever achieve. This is a simple but devastatingly important point to consider as we deliberate on who the system benefits and how it tends to do so.
2. And, it is worth noting, in environments of increasingly precarious and flexible labour markets deregulated by governments.

what should we do?

Introduction

Up to this point our discussion has offered both an explanation and analysis of some of the political arrangements and deeper influences on the politics of housing that have led to the current UK's contemporary housing crisis. Among the arguments we have put forward is that the housing crisis is best understood as a systematic set of economic and political arrangements maintained by successive governments. We have also suggested that the current crisis should not be seen as being an unintended consequence of policymaking but as a necessary feature of a system that is in place to maintain the resource base of wealthy households and investors.

In contrast to some other critical accounts, we do not frame the current housing crisis as a 'wicked problem' (see for example Gallent, 2019) that has been difficult to address because rising residential property values are seen as a measure of consumer confidence and a successful economy. Nor do we wish to convey that the housing crisis is simply due to a shortage of supply which can be easily attended to just by building more public housing. We would also add that while new public housing is essential and would play an enormous role in addressing housing need, it is not a sufficient response to the housing crisis.

Here we restate the need for a somewhat unblinking commitment in which the structural forces and enduring interests of capital are located as the primary influences on a repeated series of housing crises and the continuing ineffectiveness of government responses. The resulting impression is of a wavering set of minor victories to working households (always, it seems, ultimately illusory or short-lived) and the sustained win of capital as it galvanises voting, interest and a widespread ideological triumph that runs from the economy through to many aspects of the culture we inhabit today.

The political arrangements currently in place can be addressed through a set of interventions. This noted, we do not think there is much to be gained by proposing administrative or managerial adjustments unless these are accompanied by concerted changes that attend to the kinds of massive wealth inequities we see today focused around housing and the persistent removal of efforts to address the need for capital and the wealthy to have less in order that all households can enjoy humane living conditions. Without more systemic policies to address inequality, the reforms are likely to be at greater risk of being overturned by a new incoming government, keen to restore the privileges previously enjoyed by the well off.

Over the last three decades or so, too much time has been wasted on debating the finer points of incremental adjustments or on research inquiries that delve into one or more features of the housing system. While such administrative reforms may ameliorate some of the most abject features of housing inequality, in the longer term, the underlying arrangements will remain intact. A feature of this book is our attempt to show how the current configuration of the property machine (one much more financialised than when Ambrose and Colenutt wrote in the 1970s) maintains profit-making opportunities by enabling speculation and sustaining the persistent shortages required to make such profits attractive to capital.

As we have explained, finance, banking, property developers and real estate institutions benefit from a shortage of housing while being enabled as investors in both social and private housing. Without these conditions it would not be possible to extract such significant levels of returns from renters and first-time buyers. The resistance of these institutions to systemic reforms, or to the partial switching off or tempering of excessive profitability, is an important factor explaining why many progressive policy ideas have made such little headway.

Resisting reform in an era of austerity

The resistance of finance, real estate and politics is subtle but it is also strategic. We are told, for example, that homeownership is the natural or even 'instinctual' tenure that enables households to accumulate significant returns that will provide security. Yet much of what is presented about accessing a decent, owned home, itself a laudable prospect, has become wrapped in motives to 'win' by making a personal profit from the sale of the home at a later date, rather than focusing on affordable access to homeownership as itself a freedom from paying rent to or being intruded on by landlords (many of whom are also affluent homeowners). This privileging, in a sense, of house prices (and all that this says and does for the interests of capital) rather than the pursuit of widespread or even universal access to homes is in many ways expressive of a deeper contest – between classes and between working households and capital.

House price growth has uneven distributional affects dependent on geography and economic cycles yet much of the alignment of households with the interests in capital is precisely achieved through the lure that one can be a winner in this system – that one can make money from buying a home (getting on the ladder), renting out other houses or other kinds of investment rooted ultimately in the sale or renting of homes. This is the curious power or sedative quality of what in the UK is a property-based form of capitalism; it brings many into its mindset even where some are reluctant or uncomfortable to tread because they sense that to treat homes as assets and investments risks some broader damage to the aspiration of a decent home for all.

Some defenders of the status quo suggest that redistributive housing policies will undermine the labour market and that government should leave investment decisions affecting housing to the private sector. The arguments that UK governments should withdraw as far as possible from the economy in order to let private enterprise flourish has a long history, going as far back as the eighteenth century (Bowie, 2017). It was not until the turn of the twentieth century, Bowie notes, that any political party made the case for increased investment in public expenditure.

It is mainly public expenditure that funds welfare programmes that has been subjected to the most sustained attack. Both the Conservative Party and Liberal Democrats in the 2010 election campaign sought to frame the effects of the GFC as a consequence of profligate public expenditure in order to attack Labour's period in government. Austerity measures have become a defining feature of policymaking since the Conservatives have formed government and they have continued to justify tax cuts whenever possible as a measure to boost the UK economy, often framed using the metaphor of a prudent household seeking to live within its means.

The groups most affected by austerity are low-income households living in the poorest regions of the UK. Expenditure cuts that target welfare and local government disproportionately impact the most vulnerable, who have fewer resources to manage. At the same time as welfare cuts have been enacted the government has sought to incentivise domestic and overseas investment by enabling money to be easily raised by banks (a policy termed quantitative easing). In practice, this prioritisation of investment over and above government welfare expenditure has had a disproportionate impact on markets where demand outstrips supply.

The intensification of the housing crisis

The task for housing reform has always been necessary but we can detect new tensions and fissures within the housing system, such as the third of young adults between the ages of 18 and 34 now living with their parents (Elliot, 2019). The circling predators of international housing investment funds waiting to be granted access to buy and run public housing, or the increasing frequency of flooding, highlight the wider relationship between housing systems and an ecology damaged by unchecked capitalism. The housing crisis, which has always affected relatively poor households, is now part of the lives of many of the young middle class and limiting their opportunities. For this group, an increasingly costly education transposes neither into well-paid or secure employment nor a landscape of available housing options. Student debt, alongside household debt more generally, may yet generate part of a wider absence of ability to pay for housing that may lead to much larger house price corrections and falls.

Today, the plight of the middle classes forms the focus of increasing interest in the media and raises important questions for politics – how does the system balance the demand of an irate electorate who see housing opportunities fading with the demands of capital and owners to see continued opportunities for profit? One way, as we have suggested, is to appear to be concerned while kicking the can down the road – decisions on taxation, welfare, wages and investments in public housing moved towards some ever-retreating horizon.

We have noted that within the UK economy rising house prices are seen as a proxy for a successful economy and consumer confidence.

Most householders when they buy their home anticipate some increase in the value of their property that exceeds the cost of their investment. There is a fear that pension provision will be insufficient to meet the associated costs that accompany old age and there has been a growth of equity release financial products as a consequence of this fear. The notion of asset-based welfare has come to be a popular way of thinking about what our home is intended to deliver, in the sense of an asset that can be raided late in life to pay for the things we need as the state withdraws. This is a significantly motivating fear for those unable but desiring to enter home-ownership. In addition, there is evidence that many households see their home as not just providing for retirement but also an enabler for children and even grandchildren to manage better.

In recent years there has been a far greater expectation among households to make significant capital gains on their initial investment and the opportunities for wealth creation have encouraged both domestic and overseas landlords, as well as institutions (through sovereign wealth funds, for example), to buy properties in UK cities. In London especially, the entry of large numbers of investors has significant impacts, effectively pricing out first-time buyers without financial support from their parents. The ripple effect in house prices can be observed in locations such as central London which is now unaffordable except for the very wealthy (Minton, 2017). One consequence of a view of the housing system as a form of roulette is that in a period of falling prices there is widespread concern about how to reinstate growth, rather than seeking to address deeper housing problems.

It is not an unintended consequence of policymaking that it is only the well off who can now afford to buy homes in inner London and other sought-after cities in the south of England such as Oxford, Cambridge and Bristol. Young households with limited incomes now struggle to become homeowners. Consider for example the report by the Institute of Fiscal Studies (Cribb et al., 2018) that highlighted that for 25–34 year olds with incomes between £22,000 and £30,600, the proportion owning their home has declined from 65% in 1995–1996 to 27% in 2015–2016. Many of these households are required either to live with their parents or to pay high rents to investor landlords.

The profits that property development (both residential and commercial) can generate for investors have led to a large hike in the value of land (which is always finite in supply). The high cost of land creates an additional incentive for developers to hold off for a period of time from commencing building projects as they can expect greater gains by delaying the start of construction (a choice known as land-banking). In a period of rising land value, it is also the case that many development sites are bought and sold without any new building even being built. The government has abetted these circuits of purchase and sale by establishing a tax regime that rewards speculative forms of investment and not taking any action to curb such practices – proposals to do so come and go without action being taken.

Other developments that we can detect in the UK housing system are the extent to which many recent first-time homeowners are struggling to service the costs of their mortgage debts and tenants living in private sector accommodation who pay a large proportion of their income on rent. The high cost of housing has wider implications for the UK economy insofar as many households have less spending capacity, thereby reducing overall spending needed to maintain the economy. Of course, the most visible manifestation of the housing crisis is the number of people living rough. The national charity Shelter has estimated that there were as many as 318,000 people who experienced periods of homelessness in 2018. Action to address such problems is, however, rarely just one of housing policy.

To really improve social outcomes would take concerted action on reducing the commodification of housing, investing in public housing, taxing the purchase of homes to prevent speculation, fairer annual property tax based on land values, improving the wages and conditions of working households (but which then tend to be lost through higher rents and house prices as a result!), action on pensions to prevent funds being used to raise prices, taxes or blocks on offshore investment and money laundering, controls on rents to disincentivise investment landlords, the regulation of building to achieve better space and quality standards and environmental standards, improved relationships between health, welfare and care systems for older people, and on, and on!

Certainly, there are factors that make it difficult for governments to act, but the primary driver sustaining the crisis is the unwillingness of the political class (recognising also the complexity of arbitrating between the interests of capital and progressive reform) to address the inequities of the housing market and put in place active measures that would redistribute wealth accumulated through speculation and inheritance (which gives new generations enormous amounts of personal wealth that they have not earned and which is often held in estates and property).

Policymakers and politicians often appear to be comfortable with the idea that the housing 'problem' is too complex to be resolved and that significant intervention is likely to have damaging consequences for the economy. Casting the housing crisis as a 'wicked' problem or as being too 'complex' occludes the fundamental issue at stake; which is that the inequalities that are produced from the current housing configuration sustain ongoing opportunities for profiteering at the expense and misery of a great many households who see their lives, health, education and well-being suffer as a result.

Possibilities for reform and intervention

We have argued that it is helpful to differentiate two forms of government interventions: policies that attend to the limited supply of affordable housing (supply-side interventions) and those that focus on the individual consumer of housing (demand-side interventions). Up until the mid-1970s, supply-side responses were the main form of government activity (in the form of council housing building programmes) to attend to existing housing shortages and dilapidation. However, it is evident that the mid-1970s marked a turning point in housing policy, as governments began to switch from their supply-side investment approach towards more targeted assistance to individual households deemed to need assistance. Rental support to households in the private sector (housing benefit) and subsidies to first-time home buyers are two examples of such housing demand-side interventions.

It is worth pausing at this point to return to our discussion in Chapter 2 where we explained why this switch in housing policy took place. As we explained, the 1970s was a tumultuous period in UK politics when Labour and Conservative administrations struggled to reduce government debt, inflation and rising unemployment. Traditional Keynesian supply-side interventions that were a feature of the 1950s and 1960s were subject to a critique from economists who called for the targeting of inflation as the priority for government. Among their suggestions were the tightening of the supply of money (a policy known as monetarism), wage controls and cutting back public expenditure.

The idea underpinning monetarist-inspired economics was that such actions were necessary to 'free' the private sector and boost profitability. The shift to demand-side housing policies was part of a suite of monetarist interventions to reduce welfare expenditure and target resources in ways that were thought as being more efficient. The historical sketch we provided also explained how the failure to provide public housing in areas of high demand and high cost in the 1980s and 1990s has led to the present-day crisis which, we would acknowledge, feels even more difficult to imagine a way out of.

In this section we set out some potential policies for reform. As we have argued, the policy debate fixating on 'affordability' provides cover for the government to continue resourcing demand-side interventions in the private sector (both for owner occupation and the private rental markets) rather than address the lack of public housing in areas of acute shortage. Our proposals below are deliberately provocative and are only partly tempered by political expediencies in order to escape the tendency for continued reforms at the margins that we have tried to criticise.

1. Curbing rent seeking and speculation

It is necessary to disincentivise bank lending for speculative investment purposes, where profits are accrued on capturing future value and provide inducements for banks to lend funds for productive investment that directly contribute to GDP (Ryan-Collins et al., 2017: 208). Of course, any action such as this would be challenged by those profiting from housing shortages. Financial institutions would almost certain protest and claim that foreign investment, indeed any speculative investment, in new housing stock is beneficial as the funds eventually filter down to low-income households who are able to rent stock that is vacated when households move into the new properties. However, the evidence that this outcome eventuates is yet to be demonstrated.

Increasing supply at the high end of the market has not led to a fall in prices in periods when demand remains so high. A recent feature of the London housing market has been the large number of properties in traditional low-cost areas now being occupied by those on high incomes (such as Brixton, Peckham, Hackney and Walthamstow). Furthermore, an important point to be considered is that any investment in new buildings, as Gallent et al. point out, 'is squeezed into the same bounded space; it subtracts from the same available land supply; and it diverts demand in other sections of the market elsewhere' (2017: 2209–2210). Cities like London have been joined by others like Birmingham, Leeds, Liverpool and Manchester which have seen significant speculative capital that has tended to generate housing through 'build to rent' or which is low quality, high cost and often in one- or two-bed flats.

Nick Gallent (2019) has argued that governments must actively mediate investor demand for housing in ways that are not detrimental to the interests of those without resources or capital. The UK government has recently reduced some of the tax incentives that were on offer to landlord investors but there is much more required to reduce the appeal that housing has to offer speculative investors. For example, imposing obligations on foreign investors and international investment capital funds that prevent their capacity to buy existing housing developments. Legislation could be also enacted that only allows foreign investment in those new built developments that feature at least a 30% social housing component.

2. Curtail private landlordism

The government has reduced subsidies to private landlords and raised taxes on the purchase of second homes. This is to be welcomed as the policies were ineffectual and led to problematic outcomes. For example, 'Buy to Let' schemes have not only meant that landlords could outbid aspiring first-time homeowners, thereby acting as a break on homeownership, but also led to more properties being offered to tenants in poor condition. However, we would go far further by suggesting that governments end *any* support for all forms of private landlordism. Currently, while public housing tenants are beneficiaries of government funds that flow through to local authority housing revenue accounts, private renters have few rights and are vulnerable to eviction at short notice.

While some commentators portray housing benefit and local housing allowances as forms of subsidy to private renters, in practice these subsidies are immediately transferred to the landlord who is also able to charge higher rents in the knowledge that low-income tenants are eligible to receive government housing benefit. Measures need to be put in place to establish a more equitable distribution of funds, so that renters are not disadvantaged. The quickest way to achieve this would be to disincentivise private landlordism by imposing new tax obligations on their profits. In addition to such measures by government, it would seem worthwhile that pressure groups for renters focus their efforts on showing how many private landlords make profits by using the fixed capital resources of homes in order to expand their personal wealth. If these types of private landlords choose other, more progressive forms of social investment while exiting the sector, we could hope to see the possibility of falling prices and the use of such housing by owner occupiers.

3. Public house building

We have stressed how austerity policies that have been pursued by government since 2010 are undoubtedly a major impediment to the arguments for sustained public investment in housing. Bowie considers the Conservative/Liberal government decision in 2010 effectively to end central government investment in social housing by making a 70% cut in the investment budget of the previous Labour administration and switching funds to an affordable rent programme (Bowie, 2017: 33) to support below-market-rent (80%) housing in the housing association sector. Clearly, any government policy response must address shortage of public housing in cities such as London and other areas of high demand. And yet, while increasing the depleted supply of affordable housing in areas of high need is an important component of a serious reform agenda, it is not a sufficient response without accompanying interventions.

To fix on supply alone is tantamount to overlooking the other political interventions that are required. Of course, stating that there should be more public housing is meaningless unless accompanied by an implementation strategy. Our preference is for local authorities to take up this new building role, but we also recognise the capacity of larger 'not-for-profit' housing associations to undertake a supplementary role, on the condition that they operate in more democratic and accountable ways than has been the case in recent years. For example, there is evidence that, in London, housing association regeneration has mainly benefitted affluent households and led to the dispossession and displacement of working-class communities (Watt, 2020).

We know there is a considerable anxiety about the capacity of local authorities and not-for-profit agencies to take charge of new social housing projects. Much of this anxiety can be traced to longstanding assumptions that the responsive capabilities of not-for-profits and councils are weighed down by bureaucratic obligations. So, for example, compared with private sector companies, it is claimed that there are just too many onerous reporting mechanisms within the public and social housing sectors that impede their capacity to build. There is some basis to this claim and, certainly, the austerity cuts that have been imposed by Conservative administrations since 2010 have stretched the budgets of many local authorities to near breaking point. However, while recognising that underfunding is currently a major impediment, it is nonetheless not an insurmountable one.

An adequately resourced budget for new housing development that makes it easier for local authorities to borrow money at preferential interest rates would be required. In contrast to for-profit companies, all the investment in new housing is retained by the taxpayer rather than leaking into profits for private sector agencies. Any public sector building programme will require a major injection of resources so that local authorities have the capacity to deliver.

4. Planning reform

A rejuvenated public sector would also require effective planning instruments to ease the delivery of new stock. The UK government has been complicit in portraying local authority planning controls as an obstacle to boosting the supply of affordable housing. This is politically expedient as it shifts attention to other institutions rather than the government itself. As Bowie (2017) has argued, an important feature of the UK housing crisis is that the demand for affordable housing is uneven, with the most acute shortage in the south-east of England.

Bowie (2017: 141) has also set out how a functioning planning system can be used to tackle the UK's current housing crisis. He suggests that a first step is to assess housing need across all housing tenures and types and then determine targets to reduce shortfalls. Government funding should only be provided to housing that meets sustainability and quality standards. As he notes, 'England is the only country in Western Europe that has no national spatial plan' (p. 149). The Lyons Report on spatial planning recommended a cap on the uplift that can flow through to a landowner when land is re-zoned for housing use (Bowie, 2017: 154) so that the increase in value is largely retained by the community.

Planning legislation is one of the instruments that policymakers must use to facilitate public housing approvals and impose social housing obligations on private sector developers. This may be achieved through imposing stringent rules on developers to require them to provide a social housing component in their development. However, there is evidence that developers in areas of high market demand have been adept at overcoming local authority land use controls and planning requirements so that a proportion of new developments are offered as 'affordable housing'.

5. Nationalisation of land

The expansion of public housing will be expensive and this is due to the high cost of land, which is the largest component of construction costs. This is one of the major impediments that currently prevent local authorities from building new homes. We believe that local authorities should take steps to nationalise some land in areas of high demand to facilitate public housing development. There is also scope for local authorities to use compulsory purchases to fast-track building programmes. This was used with great effect in the 1960s and 1970s despite criticism from private landlords. The campaigning organisation Shelter (2017) has suggested that a large house building programme could be enhanced by enabling local authorities to establish development corporations for the purposes of creating new housing to ease the pressure on existing settlements.

The task of nationalising parcels of land would be difficult politically, but as Gallent (2019: 145) has pointed out, many planning measures are piecemeal and often worked around by private sector developers and landlords who successfully deploy consultants to find ways to resist any imposition for a social housing component in their development plans. Gallent does not go so far as land nationalisation but he does suggest that local authority planning authorities should distinguish between housing built for residents/family and speculative housing, and then to change the rules on capital gains tax and limit households to owning just one resident/ family house to deter developers selling stock to investors. As he explains, 'the aim with "resident/family dwelling houses" would be to bring down cost, relative to local earnings, in perpetuity, and therefore prevent the accumulation of capitalised land (realised on sale, making them potentially unaffordable to successive buyers)' (Gallent, 2019: 146–147).

There are other suggestions that should be considered such as those advanced by Parvin (2018). He proposed that local authorities could compulsorily purchase land or identify sites for development and then lease plots for land to local families or small groups of households who could then either build or buy homes for their own use. Parvin cites two examples that can serve as a prototype: Almere in the Netherlands where householders can either buy or rent plots that have pre-applied planning consent (see Feary, 2015) and the Greater London Assembley's 'small sites' portal that enables low-cost housing opportunities (GLA: 2019).

6. Environmental sustainability and building regulations

The Grenfell fire in London that took place in 2017 and the subsequent public inquiry examining its causes has led to an increased awareness of the regulatory failures within the UK housing building system. Some commentators such as Hodkinson (2019) have argued that the disaster can be considered as a symptom of a failure to fund adequately collective welfare provision over successive decades. Clearly, there is a need to establish a better resourced system of regulation to monitor and enforce building legislation. A similar challenge relates to environment standards to ensure that new housing is energy efficient and environmentally sustainable.

The government has now acknowledged the dangers posed to the population from climate change, but the mechanisms in place to address these dangers are woeful. The risks from flooding and heatwaves require resources for local government and other statutory agencies to take remedial action, but thus far the Westminster government has yet to provide the funds to address these issues. It is not just government agencies that should resource remedial action. There are good reasons to require developers, who choose to build in high-risk areas, to contribute to any compensation fund for households whose property has been damaged by flooding.

There are also wider questions about the environment and how we organise our lives during a period of rampant neoliberalism and accelerated climate change. As Simone (2016: 151) has argued, we need to pay attention to the many ways that households living in poverty have managed to forge innovative ways of living in mutually productive ways. Otherwise 'we might miss opportunities to see something else taking place, vulnerable and provisional though it might be'.

7. Tax reform

Finally, we return to the issue of taxation. A major requirement for any serious response to the UK housing crisis is to change the taxation system by distributing the gains accrued from speculative investments to the less well off or, even better, close opportunities for speculative forms of invest-ment. One way to proceed would be to establish a tax that is linked to the value of land (a land tax). Here, the UK government could draw upon the example of Singapore where 90% of the land is owned by the government (Ryan-Collins et al., 2017) but offered to private developers for develop-ment. At the end of the lease, the land is returned to the government. Such an arrangement enables the government, not the developer, to capture the rise in land values while the developer's source of profit is from the sale or rent from the new homes.

A capital gains tax on all residential property transactions (irrespective of whether a home is a principal place of residence) would help to deter speculative purchasing. However, such a policy would be firmly resisted by the banks and financial sector, both of which derive much of their profits from lending to home purchasers. Ideally, it would be a better outcome to establish a national bank. In this way, profits made from the debts incurred by borrowers would be returned to the taxpayer rather than the shareholders and executives of commercial banks.

Though likely to be met with opposition, a carefully designed sys-tem of death taxes on housing wealth could also help fund a new public housing programme and avoid many of the problems associated with inheritance tax, which is often avoided by many of the richest families who carefully plan the inheritance of their wealth.

There is also a role for local authorities as forms of housing inequal-ity and exclusion could be addressed by stronger local taxation – a much wider and progressive A–Z banding of council tax for example, to differenti-ate varying price advantages and local amenity advantages. The proceeds from these council taxes could also be used to provide much needed assistance to the many low-income households who have to endure poor conditions in the private rental sector. There are other issues that require action – currently there are insufficient incentives to entice owners of prop-erties standing empty to let their homes. Doubling council tax, for example, would provide a good incentive for owners to utilise their property.

We would also advocate a far higher tax on second homes to free up properties that are mainly purchased by wealthy households for weekend breaks from London and other large conurbations. This would make up for the significant tax revenue shortfalls for local councils who have a large number of properties classed as holiday homes (see Iqbal, 2018). There are other impacts: for example, many young local residents in villages where second home properties are a feature are having to live with their parents or move out of their neighbourhood. Second homes also have other impacts: they are often empty and it is quite common for occupiers to stock up supplies and groceries before arriving and so add little to the local economy.

Similarly, tighter restrictions on Airbnb and other web-based platforms are required to increase the stock available for long-term tenancies, which are often bought to be used as short-term lets, often in cities with intensive tourism that competes with local residents for the use of these homes.

Conclusion: The politics of implementation

Here we have offered what many will believe to be unthinkable, unworkable and perhaps outrageous proposals. Yet these build on the ideas of many working in the housing studies community devoted to the question of how to improve conditions and indeed to tackle the inequalities that are so starkly expressed in relation to personal housing wealth, or the creation of wealth through housing investment. We have provided both a diagnosis and some of the necessary policy interventions that might help to attend to the core of the housing crisis. In this chapter we have alluded to some of the practical ways that interventions might be progressed.

Reforms would undoubtedly be met with fierce resistance, including behind the scenes lobbying and media campaigns by those who would stand to lose their existing entitlements. We would expect, for example, banks and mortgage lenders to warn that reforms would undermine the economy, developers to suggest that housing affordability issues would intensify, and real estate agencies and landlord lobbyists to argue that renters would risk homelessness. Politically, it would be difficult for any political party to campaign for reforms that could easily be construed as an attack on the wealth opportunities of homeowners. The best opportunity for the reforms we have advocated would be for legislation passed by a confident left-of-centre political party with a large majority in Parliament (as was the case in 1945). However, given the parlous state of UK politics this seems unlikely, at least for the immediate future.

A necessary way forward is for those interested in effective and sustainable methods to generate decent homes for all to advance reasoned, evidenced and dispassionate cases for fundamental reform. Of course, these campaigns will be attacked as unworkable and damaging to the economy. Such reforms would be construed as an attack on the British way of life, of being ideologically motivated or as examples of the 'politics of envy'. It is unrealistic to expect the wealthy simply to give up on the privileges that are currently in place – yet in some cases the contradictions even here are opening up as the middle classes see their own children as victims of an intensifying financialised housing system, unable to buy, struggling to rent and seeing their futures as increasingly precarious. Such systemic limits may yet tilt larger numbers to lobby and act in favour of those who work for a living rather than those who live from the placing of investment bets.

We predict that the stark inequalities that make up the contemporary UK political and economic context will eventually be addressed, not least because aggregate demand in the economy is too reliant on unsustainable and huge levels of personal indebtedness. There is little prospect of a right-wing political party taking such steps because it embodies the interests of the wealthy and capital. Despite this we may again see contradictions opening up as some with more market-oriented dispositions recognise the social antagonism and disruptions that the raw force of capital is generating. Models of more inclusive capitalism, social investment, the development of a more ecological consciousness and recognition of the limits of inequality are beginning here to be in evidence. Nevertheless, the most likely instrument for eventual reform will require left-wing parties to establish a 'Housing' Royal Commission and accept the recommendations proposed.

The Westminster adversarial style of politics lends itself to short-term policy fixes, so fashioning a long-term policy intervention that might limit opportunities for future governments to reverse progressive change will be a major challenge. One lesson from the Right to Buy programme is that new legislation will be required to safeguard societal benefits that would flow from new public housing investment. Yet the real promise of such reforms would be immense because they would establish an invigorated housing system designed to meet the shelter and human developmental requirements of households universally, rather than enabling the continued existence of an alienating housing system that exists to maintain the profits of the already wealthy. This would be a major step for establishing a fairer and more equal society and a more stable economic future.

5

conclusion

In this book we have tried to enable readers to see the crisis in housing as the result of a tension between the political and economic realms, embodied in what we have called the property machine, and their opposition to the social and everyday needs of the majority of the population. In this short conclusion we set out some closing reflections on the relevance of viewing housing in this way, what such a viewpoint reveals, and how our diagnosis might be of value for those interested in advancing a programme that leads to improved housing conditions for all.

To restate our initial working premise, there is very little to be gained from a view that sees discussion of house building numbers, interest rates and the dream of ownership as anything other than a facade that conceals the persistent features of a property-driven economy. Behind that facade exist a series of powerful interests who appear to identify the root of the problem or to offer solutions but who, if anything, have only further cemented their wealth and market advantages. Governments persist in handwringing talk of lost hopes, a broken housing system and recognition of the stress of many, but this belies a massive lack of momentum for more concerted action, because to do so would challenge the combined interests of banks, house builders, financiers and landlord investors. High private profit rates, 'lucky' homeowners, homelessness, pitiful construction standards and a lack of sufficient supply are the 'healthy' signs that this dysfunctional context persists.

We have observed, in line with the analysis of many others, that the housing crisis is a persistent feature of a system that, at its roots, is tied to a market orientation that sees the need to placate and provide for capital. In this context, wealthy individuals and key institutions have continued to do well and buck the trend facing many in terms of real declines in living conditions, material hardship and poor-quality homes. Public housing has been denigrated and viewed as an unenviable 'product' for investment by the state. Support for homelessness services is much needed, not simply to deal with those who are homeless – much more substantive programmes are required that attend to such problems that highlight pronounced inefficiencies and market failures. These failures interact with wider social losses and precariousness presided over by government in the domains of employment, education and social justice.

Housing is implicated in a broad set of social, economic and political forces. The advantage of understanding this is that we can then see how housing is capable of being set in service of human need through new forms of organisation, regulation and policymaking. Supportive interventions by governments, effective programmes and policies (rent controls, public housing construction, land value taxes, reducing incentives and subsidies for capital) at other times and in other countries highlight what can be achieved.

Unlike earlier housing-related crises the general predicaments we have outlined are fundamentally linked to an increasingly turbocharged mode of capitalism that assigns financial values even to social infrastructure, notably public housing, but also creates further tradable and investable instruments on the back of this. This process can be seen in other areas (like proposals to sell student loan debt) but in housing it is perhaps clearest. The most recent and nearly system-breaking financial crisis enfolded multiple institutions and countries around the world. That crisis was the culmination of the complex interconnection of housing debt (mortgage-backed securities) and the arrogance and aggressive use of such instruments to drive profits and ignore important risks. Yet such predatory and irresponsible characteristics that underlie market-oriented societies are resurgent and again risk the further destabilisation of an already vulnerable global economic system. Forces of international capital and speculation are ready, including BlackRock or Blackstone, seeking new markets in which to extract profit from social housing portfolios in the UK and in other countries. The role of the state to control and check these forms of excess is clearly needed.

Where can we go from here? What is to be made of a system that we know to be so damaging and deficient and yet which seems to offer such important gains and advantages to so many? Criticism is challenging where capitalism and the housing system have made many property millionaires, delivering real wealth and even psychological benefits to many. A deep and perhaps unassailable conservatism arises when the system may seem only half broken or capable of being reformed in some way. This is a kind of false hope that helps to head off more trenchant criticism of the pension funds, the offshore billionaires, the lax regulatory regime, the absence of challenges to developers wishing to evade social housing contributions and the generation renting from another generation.

All of this highlights what is at stake for entire industries whose interests are wrapped up in something that looks like the status quo or which indeed might help to generate even greater profits by encouraging forms of privatisation, sales of public land and the 'de-risking' of such programmes by governments who have shown how committed they are to market principles even where these continue to let down large numbers of people. Of course, the problem here, the contradiction at the heart of such a system, is that these benefits to a minority are connected to a broader situation in which many others are left wanting or indeed bereft.

All of this leads us back in many ways to the same problems that Engels identified in his analysis of the 'housing question' more than a century ago. We might wish to assume that policymakers, banks and developers are fundamentally committed to resolving the core questions today – how can we help everyone to be safe, happy and affordably housed in ways that allow all of those myriad areas of their social lives to be enriched and enabled? We must not be so naive as to think that such groups are willing or even capable (beholden as they are to constituencies and shareholders) of doing so.

Enormous public effort and conversation are required – built from an understanding of the two core forces (property on the one hand, social on the other) and demands built upon this understanding for clearer alternatives to be created and implemented. But such work is hard and will be seen as assailing deep and longstanding beliefs, even among those who are critical of the system's excesses and failures – renters wish to become owners, those with money seek to invest and for it to grow, owners make demands on governments for low interest rates, and so on. Such beliefs help erode momentum for the kinds of action we have tried to offer in this book.

Far from a politics of envy we need to point out how an engrained politics of self-interest around which many groups, individuals and institutions are strongly mobilised continues to operate. However, we also need to understand how such motives are often fuelled by real fears – of the loss of income in retirement and of providing for offspring who may face their own challenges. Such fears thrive in a competitive social and economic context in which a dwindling state supports a precarious labour market and the promises previously associated with education are increasingly evident. The role of the state as a source of combined action on behalf of a national community is critical to arbitrating and achieving momentum to tackle the core human requirement of a safe, affordable and secure home.

There is now growing anger and increasing evidence of action to address many of the problems we have identified in this short book. Those who take a dialectical view of history (in which extreme forms of social and political action end up inducing counter-reactions) may think that social progress may be encouraged by these problems. The massive privatisations, gifts to offshore and financialised capital, the wholesale defunding, stigmatisation and demolition of public housing, rising homelessness – all of these accelerating shifts, erosions of public support that might offset the excessive demands of capital – will likely see attempts at creating a fairer system if not perhaps revolutionary action, which very few would wish to see. Yet the real breakthrough today is the way in which research has shown how the world of offshore finance is actually having the effect of making the world of the rich, the banks and so on more available to scrutiny. The bad news is that there is an incredibly long way to go! Nevertheless, traction on the question of unfairness, inequality and private excess seems assured as further revelations and investigations appear.

For everyday households supply–demand imbalances, the planning system or whether another property bubble is coming are not immediate concerns. These are the issues that politicians, financiers and developers are primarily interested in. Yet we have argued in this book that to tool up everyday thinking about the contemporary housing problem requires us to look more deeply than the daily froth of such commentary. For the groups concerned with these issues are indeed those with vested interests – in political stability and electoral gain, in securing continuing and expanding profits, and in moderating supply in order to underwrite returns. Often, such interests are presented within a powerful economic narrative that sees change or reform as a threat to national well-being when in reality the threat is often to sectional and wealthy interests. It is neither cynical nor inaccurate to suggest that these deep and powerful interests come to act through the realm of the political domain and that the desire for wealth creation pursued in this way widens inequalities and leaves questions of market failure unaddressed.

As we write, we note that five years of the Help to Buy policy have seen £12.5 billion spent on this programme (2013–2019); it is widely understood to have inflated prices and pushed many buyers to the limit of what they can afford. The policy has appeared to do good by new and less well-off households wanting the relative security of owning, and yet in reality most buyers using the scheme could have afforded to borrow what they did in any case. Such policies highlight the deep interests of governments in helping to secure gains to capital even as many people who think they benefit has, in reality, primarily helped the owners of development companies and those with shareholders in them. Enormous profitability has been helped by what was presented as a form of state aid to the less well off. So, on one level we might criticise this policy for having unintended effects, helping the better off and inflating prices. Alternatively, in line with the analysis we have offered in this book, we might see instead that the policy worked very much as intended.

In focusing on our own domestic context, the UK, we are nevertheless drawn into a globally pervasive system of political interests and economic structures. The global economic system is one set in pursuit of continuing growth, an essential characteristic of capitalism. To talk about the UK's problem is necessarily to talk about other scales and processes that impact upon us. Reform of a property-based economy does not require the abolition of private property but rather its more equitable sharing – for the system to work more effectively, those with so much would need to have less, and this is increasingly a compelling moral case as the extent of income, wealth and land inequalities are revealed to us.

Reform does not mean that owners should become renters, or that renters should give up on seeking to become owners. What is required is a more neutral policy environment in which a more level playing field allows private choices and opportunities to facilitate movement between renting and owning while dampening the use of housing as an asset to leverage greater wealth. The acceptance of this 'cost' and the reforms that would need to be put in place would probably not be possible without a considerable reorientation of political debate and some soul searching more generally in search of a fairer society. But instead of starting with private owners and the middle classes we would do better to begin by curtailing the interests of capital (which generates benefits in the form of pensions and investments to the mostly wealthy) and to advance housing provisions in the form of accountable and professionally managed social housing.

Our current fixation with the wealth opportunities that can accrue from homeownership is perhaps the biggest barrier to ending the housing crisis. Clearly, the link between profit and housing must be broken so that the home can provide a stable, steady-state tenure. We acknowledge that to break this link would require changes in public attitudes to what the role of ownership is and should be: the need to move from a mindset fixed on the prospect of personal wealth creation to one in which the core social function of home is celebrated – the house as a place to live rather than an investment. In essence, this means that the use and need for increasing amounts of private finance should be reduced while the state's role in providing a high-quality, affordable, secure and well-managed public sector should be expanded. Such an option might seem more attractive if, as in earlier periods, this was met with proposals to use public infrastructure spending to deploy private builders to construct these public homes. Without action we will remain stuck in a system that requires households to chase dreams of ownership, wealth and personal security in a system rigged primarily to provide opportunities for investors rather than those in social need.

references

Ambrose, P. & Colenutt, B. (1975) *The Property Machine*, Harmondsworth: Penguin.

Bowie, D. (2017) *Radical Solutions to the Housing Crisis*, Bristol: Policy Press.

Brignall, M. (2019) 'Average UK household debt now stands at record £15,400', *Guardian*, 7 January, www.theguardian.com/business/2019/jan/07/average-uk-household-debt-now-stands-at-record-15400 (accessed 22 October 2019).

Collinson, P. (2019) 'Boris Johnson and the housing crisis', *Guardian*, 2 August, www.theguardian.com/politics/2019/aug/02/boris-johnson-and-the-housing-crisis (accessed 4 September 2019).

Cribb, J., Hood, A. & Hoyle J. (2018) *The Decline of Homeownership Among Young Adults*, London: Institute of Fiscal Studies. www.ifs.org.uk/uploads/publications/bns/BN224.pdf (accessed 29 October 2019).

Department of Communities and Local Government, UK (2017) *Fixing our Broken Housing Market*, Cmnd. 9532, London: HMSO.

Department of the Environment, UK (1971) *A Fair Deal for Housing*, Cmnd. 4728, London: HMSO.

Dunleavy, P. (1981) *The Politics of Mass Housing in Britain 1945–1975: A Study of Corporate Power and Professional Influence in the Welfare State*, Oxford: Clarendon.

Elliot, L. (2019) 'The demise of the middle class is toxifying politics', *Guardian*, 3 May, www.theguardian.com/commentisfree/2019/may/03/demise-middle-classes-british-politics-digital-age (accessed 29 September 2019).

Engels, F. (1872/1975) *The Housing Question*, Moscow: Progress Publishers.

Feary, T. (2015) 'Inside Almere: The Dutch city that's pioneering alternative housing', *Guardian*, 15 December, www.theguardian.com/housing-network/2015/dec/15/almere-dutch-city-alternative-housing-custom-build (accessed 26 August 2019).

Gallent, N. (2019) *Whose Housing Crisis? Assets and Homes in a Changing Economy*, Bristol: Policy Press.

Gallent, N., Durrant, D. & May, N. (2017) 'Housing supply, investment demand and money creation: A comment on the drivers of London's housing crisis', *Urban Studies*, 54 (10), 2204–2216.

Greater London Assembly (GLA) (2018) *Affordable Housing Monitor*, www.london. gov.uk/about-us/london-assembly/london-assembly-publications/affordable-housing-monitor-20172018 (accessed 3 September 2019).

Greater London Assembly (GLA) (2019) 'Small Sites', Mayor of London, London Assembly, https://www.london.gov.uk/what-we-do/housing-and-land/land-and-development/small-sites (accessed 26 August 2019).

Harloe, M. (1995) *The People's Home: Social Rented Housing in Europe and America*, Oxford: Blackwell.

Harvey, D. (2010) *The Enigma of Capital*, London: Profile.

Hodkinson, S. (2019) *Safe as Houses: Private Greed, Political Negligence and Housing Policy After Grenfell*, Manchester: Manchester University Press.

Hoskens, A. (2007) *Nothing Like a Dame: The Scandals of Shirley Porter*, London: Granta.

Iqbal, N. (2018) 'Are holiday homes ruining the British seaside?', *Guardian*, 19 August, https://www.theguardian.com/money/2018/aug/19/are-holiday-homes-ruining-uk-seaside (accessed 26 August 2019).

Johnson, B. (2018) Speech at the Conservative Party Conference, October, https://blogs.spectator.co.uk/2018/10/full-text-boris-johnsons-tory-fringe-speech/ (accessed 3 September 2019).

Malpass, P. & Murie, A. (1994) *Housing Policy and Practice*, 4th Edition, Basingstoke: Macmillan.

Malpass, P. & Victory, C. (2010) 'The modernisation of social housing in England', *International Journal of Housing Policy 10* (1) 3–18.

Minton, A. (2017) *Big Capital: Who is London For?*, London: Penguin.

Murie, A. (2016) *The Right to Buy: Selling off Public and Social Housing*, Bristol: Policy Press.

Murie, A. (2018) 'Shrinking the state in housing: Challenges, transitions and ambiguities', *Cambridge Journal of the Regions, Economy and Society*, 11, 485–501.

Parvin, A. (2018) 'Affordable land would mean affordable housing: Here's how we get there', *Guardian*, 23 October.

Pawson, H. & Mullins, D. (2010) *After Council Housing: Britain's New Social Landlords*, London: Macmillan.

Piketty, T. (2014) *Capital in the 21st Century*, Cambridge, MA: Harvard University Press.

Powell, R. & Robinson, D. (2019) 'Housing, ethnicity and advanced marginality in England', in *Class, Ethnicity and State in the Polarized Metropolis*, pp. 187–212. London: Palgrave Macmillan.

Raco, M. (2013) 'The new contractualism, the privatization of the welfare state, and the barriers to open source planning', *Planning Practice and Research*, 28 (1), 45–64.

Rees-Mogg, J. & Tylecote, R. (2019) 'Raising the roof', Institute of Economic Affairs, London, https://iea.org.uk/publications/raising-the-roof/ (accessed 3 September 2019).

Ryan-Collins, J., Lloyd, D. & Macfarlane, L. (2017) *Rethinking the Economics of Land and Housing*, London: Zed Books.

Schumacher, P. (2018) 'Only capitalism can solve the housing crisis', Adam Smith Institute, London, 25 April, www.adamsmith.org/capitalismcansolvethe housingcrisis (accessed 26 August 2019).

Shaxson, N. (2018) *The Finance Curse: How Global Finance is Making Us All Poorer*, London: Bodley Head.

Shelter (2017) 'Consultation Response to the Department of Communities and Local Government White Paper', https://england.shelter.org.uk/professional_resources/policy_and_research/policy_library/policy_library_folder/consultation_response_fixing_the_broken_housing_market (accessed 27 August 2019).

Simone, A. (2016) 'The uninhabitable: In between collapsed yet still rigid distinctions', *Cultural Politics*, *12* (2), 135–150.

Turner, C. (2019) 'Utopian about the present', *London Review of Books*, *41* (3), 34–35.

Turner, G. (2018) 'Revealed: London council took on financial risk of estate development', *Guardian*, 12 September, www.theguardian.com/cities/2018/sep/12/london-council-aylesbury-estate-development-southwark-financial-risk (accessed 29 September 2019).

Watt, P. (2020) *Estate Regeneration and its Discontents: Public Housing, Place and Inequality in London*, Bristol: Policy Press.

Wellings, F. (2006) *British Housebuilders: History and Analysis*, Oxford: Wiley-Blackwell.

index